I0555439

**PURE
SLUSH
BOOKS**

real

stories true

Pure Slush Vol. 3

real is edited by Matt Potter and
originally published by Pure Slush, October 2012.
Second edition published October 2014.

Pure Slush Books
4 Warburton Street
Magill SA 5072
Australia
Email: edpureslush@live.com.au
Website: http://pureslush.webs.com
Visit the Pure Slush Store: http://pureslush.webs.com/store.htm

Cover photograph (New York City, June 2012) copyright © Matt Potter.

ISBN: 978-1-925101-90-4

Pure Slush proudly features (both online and in print) writers from all over the
English-speaking world. Some speak and write English as their first language,
while for others, it's their second or third or even fourth language. Naturally,
across all versions of English, there are differences in punctuation and spelling,
and even in meaning. These differences are reflected in the stories *Pure Slush*
publishes, and it accounts for any differences in punctuation, spelling and
meaning found within these pages.

non-fiction by

Gessy Alvarez	William Henderson
Cheri Ause	Gill Hoffs
Meghan K. Barnes	Claire Ibarra
Layla Blackwell	Joanne Jagoda
Laura Bogart	Maude Larke
John Wentworth Chapin	Michael Gillan Maxwell
Rebecca Chekouras	S.B. Phoenix
James Claffey	Matt Potter
Joanna Delooze	Mark Rosenblum
Mira Desai	Shane Simmons
Gloria Frym	D.M. Simone
S.H. Gall	Jonathan Slusher
Cinda Gibbon	Sharon Louise Stephenson
Walter Giersbach	Thomas Sullivan
Jane Hammons	Susan Tepper
	Diana J. Wynne

for

Ali Ayliffe

M.P.

Contents

facts

Introduction

Just over 24 hours ago, I returned to Australia from a three-month trip travelling overseas. And at the risk of sounding like a braggart, in those three months I visited the U.S. and Canada, then Portugal and Spain, France, Belgium, England and Scotland, Germany, and the Czech Republic. So a lot of miles – or kilometres in my case – were covered, on land and mid-air.

Among the many highlights of this trip was meeting many of the writers whose work has appeared in *Pure Slush*, both online and in print. Some of those I met are included in this anthology.

And for most of this trip, the weather was pleasant, sunny and warm, sometimes hot – cool in Scotland, but hey, that's Scotland! – but here, back home in southern Australia in late August, it's still winter: cold and grey and wet and dispiriting.

As a child I preferred the brace of winter to the exhaustion of summer, but now, in my mid-forties, I certainly suffer the winter blues. Just the approach of cold weather (April in Australia) is enough to send me searching for alternatives – summer in Europe, Berlin in particular! – but finances and a personal family life in Australia get in the way of an annual pilgrimage. (I know it's ridiculous: how can I change the weather?!)

So this is where *real: Pure Slush Vol. 3* comes in handy ...

Non-fiction is cheaper than travel. It takes you into other worlds and realms and lives, and just as long as the pages keep turning, your own life – or apparent lack of one – can be forgotten.

You'll find trips into art and culture, travel and food, time and the media, all within these pages.

Life should be embraced, weather permitting or not, but sometimes just a glimpse into the lives and experiences of others is enough to keep you going – and hoping – 'til better opportunities, or better weather, come along.

Matt Potter,
editor, Pure Slush, August 2012

family

Beholden

by Mira Desai

Today it's your birthday again, and you'd have been a hundred twelve, a hundred twelve like some giant banyan tree sending off tenacious roots deep into the ground, a subterranean crisscrossing that held the tree anchored so it could soar tall.

That stiff—as—hardboard back and penetrating eyes moved to another plane at ninety—one.

Ninety—one! I think of you and see you in our ancestral village home, the mud walls thick and soothing, the floor of the kitchen—front parlor—dining—living room worn stone cool with a hundred years of living. You're seated on the swing, the *jhoola* varnished by age, your hands creasing and re—creasing the pleats on your perfectly starched *dhoti*, your face aglow with a strange mix of pride—joy. A grand—son accepted at prestigious college, aye. A granddaughter chips away at another glass ceiling, aye. Overhead the ancient fan creaked, if at all, for power outages were and still are a norm.

All these years since you've been gone, with the intermixing gene line and branches of family so scattered, new bloodlines admixed, new cultural moorings – soon these stories will be forgotten, but they must not. In a village with less than six thousand, how did you dream these dreams? One man dreamt and changed the fate lines of so many... a scale change, a chance for the better. Else I'd be filling water at the well, a huddle of bawling children scrambling at my feet.

You'd wanted to pack up and go to Africa right after your LCPS, that British medical degree of the pre—independence days, but a stepmother as tough as the shrew of fairy tales ensured you'd stay in the village of the forefathers and offer prayers at their final rites. "Else their ashes will be cold before he returns," she'd scoffed, and proceeded to make your life, and your young bride's, pure hell.

Even in that dusty one—lane town, your diagnosis was unerring, no blood tests, no diagnostic tools aided your findings. Well in your seventies I remember how you'd peered through rheumy eyes and through sound and touch diagnosed a critical appendicitis with just time to breathe, aye, in due course, that child who made it to foreign university, our infotech man.

You transmitted your ambition to your children, your six—strong brood, pushed to schooling in the next town, commuting in all seasons by the only train, a slow one, or a bus that moved only when jam—packed, leaving from the village at daybreak and returning at nightfall. The parent had told me so often of playing marbles to while away the hours after school, or hungrily waiting at the station, a peanut—cone made to last an hour, and how they'd rush past the graveyard, coming home. And how he'd once leapt from the fourth—storey terrace evading a chaser, or flying kites, fractured his leg on the hard landing, but had dared not speak up, his whining at night quickly met with a cuff and brusque treatment.

We grandchildren were indulged, you'd mellowed, you'd proven your point, your obduracy had changed the life—scape, you could breathe. I was your favorite grandchild, allowed all

18

liberties, pampered at all hours of the day or night. Reserved for us were the best mangoes and the patiently re–told Mahabharata tales. For all that, I remember being envious of all the other cousins you were proud of, each medal or certificate a notch on your belt; not living up to family expectations was not even an option. No one ran away with a good–for–nothing, no hobos, no tramps, no one embezzled the bank. We still dare not.

You scoured the only newspaper that reached the village, one copy shared between eight households, pulled out opportunities from thin air. Mota kaka, elder uncle, was sent off to Dufferin at ten, to prepare for a life at sea, the spit and polish of training ship a far call from the life the rustic boys had encountered so far, raiding mango trees on picnics and skinny–dipping in streams. After futile attempts at science, flight engineering, and automobiles, the parent finally found his calling with accountancy, but to imagine in that hamlet a "Member of the Institute of Chartered Accountants of England and Wales" was a leap far out of this galaxy. A cost accountant, and yet another uncle took to the law, the brightest of the lot opted for defence services after a degree from the University of Bombay and all the world at his feet. Yes, your independent streak and *cussed persistence* burned bright in the next line, and I fervently pray it survives.

Money was tight. "Ba would send Nathu, the dispenser, to collect dues. Shrewd merchants would pay pennies on the rupee, or barter wheat or rice, he'd pilfer his share, and give her scraps. Yet she managed," lawyer uncle, now eighty–five, had said last week, the long distance line cackling with his words.

Yes, you managed, you put your head down and went on with it, despite. In my mind's eye I see sunlight touch and smoothen the creases on your face, I hear the rhythmic creak of that front–room swing and *thaap* of your foot on stone, and I struggle for the words to say thank you.

19

Immortality, Version 2.0

by Walter Giersbach

My family treated their ancestors the way you might set extra places at table. My mother and grandmother passed along centuries–old advice and anecdotes about the Fisks, Ballous, Pierces, Hastings and Drapers at the kitchen sink as though it was something they'd seen on the Six O'clock News. ("Yes," one would exclaim, "William set a trap to catch the thief stealing his firewood. He told the children he'd drilled the wood and put gunpowder inside. Of course, children can't keep a secret...." Or, "The worst thing great–great–great grandpa Ezra's third wife would say is, 'Well, I *pity* him.'")

My ancestors hover in the household like so many ghosts enjoying a summer vacation.

I'm descended from a New England family whose maternal forebears emigrated from England in the 1600s. Because of this, I'll let you know that New Englanders really do "use it up and wear it out" before anything is discarded. I've had a lot of their trunks to unpack, boxes to sort through and albums to review. It's not unusual now to straighten up a room and stop to examine Great Grandpa Ballou's letters from Fort Barrancas when he was with his Vermont Regiment, read postcards from Grandma Ballou invariably taking a train to another town where she'd lecture, or trip over the toleware candle sconces Great–Great–Grandfather Ezra Pierce played with as a child in 1816.

It's more unsettling to look at the hair collection. These are snippets of hair collected in the 19th century from the family members who had passed on. They were carefully woven, knotted and tied in bows as keepsakes. Each is identified on cards by name and dates bracketing their life. While the cardboard is disintegrating, the hair might have come from sweeping up a barbershop floor yesterday. This is not the sort of thing I can carry to the Antiques Road Show, so they've all gone into a single large envelope labeled "HAIR", waiting for my children or grandchildren to decide what to do with this memorabilia of mortality.

My limited religious ruminations stop at the thought that we remain immortal until our last acquaintance passes on. Death isn't abrupt, but it does catch up eventually. Given this dollar–store theology, I opt for saying you're "alive" until you're no longer remembered by anyone. (It might help to have some rural legends, like firewood theft prevention, to pass along for posterity.)

I'll give proper due to statues in the town square collecting bird droppings and the tombstones moldering in the marble orchard. But I can also suggest the World Wide Web is an option for immortality.

Grandmother Fisk, for example, had been a lecturer on the Chautauqua Circuit in the first decades of the 20th century, traveling the country as America's Foremost Cartoonist. She drew pastel sketches while narrating her stories — patriotic, humorous and historic — before small–town audiences. Then, the page was torn off, and she'd begin another narrative. By idly Googling her name, I discovered the University of Iowa had an extensive digital collection of Chautauqua information. I called the archivist at the U of I libraries, who exclaimed, "We had the notes and programs and schedules, but we had no idea what the actual *content* of the programs involved!" I was happy to donate her papers, photos, lecture notes and stories, which are now online. Even better, I like to think she's been given a new lease on life as students research women's liberation and write their master's theses.

I brought her father back to life as well with a piece of "true fiction." Grandmother Fisk would tell me stories when I was a child curled up in her four–poster bed. One recollection was about a famous song to come out of the Civil War, "Tenting Tonight on the Old Camp Ground". This song made the name of its composer, Walter Kittredge, known all over our country. Kittredge would visit her father — my Great–Grandpa Ballou — and together they'd sing "Tenting Tonight". The warmth of the "tent" formed by Grandma's canopied bed and all those memories can still comfort me. And perhaps even comfort her spirit if she's sitting on the bedpost. Just possibly, my great–grandfather, a loyal Union soldier, would also have a tear in his eye while tucked in snugly on the Web.

Long–dead ancestors have all come back as living memories to new generations, as alive as personalities as they were when the ladies chatted about them in the kitchen. I'm looking now at an ambrotype portrait of my great–grandmother as a child in 1859. In her penciled memoir, Mary Ballou wrote in the third person, "At 3 years of age her first picture was taken by a traveling photographer, Lawrence by name. She sat in a borrowed high chair, belonging to Charlie Jones [a neighbor child]. Black it was with white line trimmings & a diagram on the back. Her dress was pale orange with little white diamond patterns, low neck, short sleeves, and Mary was half afraid, but altogether curious to see the man put his head under a black cloth. Mother was ill with typhoid fever, and Mary was recovering from the same."

Little Charlie Jones died from typhoid shortly afterwards, and I wonder who remembers him. He never delivered a speech or wrote a letter, nor had his likeness captured in an ambrotype. Just a tombstone marks his passing, or a postscript on his parents' marker, that makes small claim to his "immortality."

Those New Englanders who never threw anything away? Mary saved a swatch of her dress. More than 150 years later, the pale orange still has an otherworldly glow as I show it to my grandchildren.

Our poignant search for unfading, eternal life compels us to store school photos, snapshots and Daguerreotypes. Those "Kodak moments" are a way to store time in a bottle. The Internet now gives them greater universality.

We can waltz through a live—for—the—moment future till the devil demands his due. Then the words of the dead become precious commodities. But there's good news. Our images and words can be archived, repeated and shared. Their spirits can be invited to the dinner table.

spreading from the false fly

by James Claffey

I sleep on my back in my childhood bedroom. The light fixture showers me with the dried flowers from my father's grave. The day he died, a light freeze covered the neglected lawn outside the ward window; the blades curved with the weight of the frozen water, like discarded ribs from Sunday's roast. A bowl of fruit stood beside his steel–framed hospital bed, despite his three weeks of unconsciousness. He unpeeled a greenish banana; looked at me with his good eye, and said, "Don't feel guilty for not being here when I died."

"Fear no more the heat of the sun," my teacher said in our literature seminar. My father stood ankle–deep in the cold Atlantic water, his trunks speckled with salt residue, his cheeks puffed out, his body intact and goosebumps all over his bare skin. I chose to ignore his attempts to communicate with me— "When are you going to settle down? Are you putting money away for a down–payment? What happened to that lovely girl you were seeing?" (She had an affair with the stockroom boy at the Pier One where she worked). The subtly put advice he tried to give me went unanswered. After the class ended, I checked my phone messages and learned how a series of mini–strokes had left him without color and with one foot in Charon's ferry.

24

After a long flight from LAX to Heathrow, and a connecting one to Dublin, I watched the flashing screen of the payphone as the coins dropped. Three rings. My mother's voice. "Ah, he died this morning at six, as the sun was coming up." I sat amongst the haphazard travelers and their carry−on bags. Three cups of strongly brewed coffee; and in the cup, the spiraling sand dunes and sharp−edged marram grass, summer holidays in thatched cottages, the memory of his laugh.

What I remember of the drive to the funeral home was the dead bugs embedded in the radiator grille of the rental car—moths, butterflies, an early wasp, and a mayfly. My father tied his own flies for fishing—a real knack. By the banks of the River Boyne he wristed the bamboo rod back−and−forth, the soft ripples spreading from the false fly, ever outward, to where he stood in his waders at the water's edge, dead at eighty−three, patiently waiting for answers.

Fairytale

by Laura Bogart

The first—and last—time I ever asked my father about God, I was eight years old and he'd had two drinks too many. I waited until the closing jingle of the six o'clock news (that was the safest time to ask him anything—we knew better than to interrupt the five day forecast) before telling him about the boy in my class who'd found presents addressed to him from Santa in his parents' closet. A slap of his thigh welcomed me on his lap.

"Daddy," I said. "Is Santa real?"

Daddy is such a sweet, tiny word; it's a candy that dissolves in your mouth. For a moment, his eyes softened like he might say something that would let me hold on to Christmas Eves with my mother, sampling cookies in the Italian bakery and picking the ones that would go well with Santa's chocolate milk.

"No," he answered as if I'd asked for ice cream for dinner. "But let's not tell your mom I told you; I love those cookies."

Sometimes, I tell this story as a joke; I cycle through his voice and a pipsqueak version of myself as a child, asking if there's an Easter Bunny and a Tooth Fairy.

"There's no Easter Bunny, and we can tell your mother I told you that because I'm sick of chewing those damn carrots," he says.

"You remember that time your mother told you that the dog scared off the Tooth Fairy, and that's why she didn't leave fifty cents under your pillow? I forgot to do it that time," he says.

"Daddy? Is there a God?"

"Nope."

It's not quite "our nada who art in nada, nada be thy name," but it's a perfect punchline.

I always end there. I never say what I wanted to know after losing Santa Claus and the Easter Bunny and the Lord Himself.

"Then why do I have to be good?"

I've auditioned many takes on his response in my head. When I want to believe that he doesn't mean it, I play it broad. Most times, I know better. I simply hear his voice—eerily affable, like he's explaining why our neighbor's car engine won't turn over:

"Because I'll beat the hell out of you."

He would become far larger and infinitely more powerful than the God he killed off. His vengeance was tidal; his forgiveness was the first flush of sun after a storm. Its magnanimous warmth lulled me into forgetting that I wasn't the one who'd sinned. I feared his anger and craved his love—even when I came to hate him. *Especially* when I came to hate him. I'd press my fingers into the bruises under my clothes, and as the shock of pain subsided into a slow, voluptuous ache, I lifted out of myself—away from the droning of my teachers; away from the kids on the bus who mocked me for walking so funny; away from my mother's cheerful nattering about keeping our grades up and our

27

voices low. It never brought me peace, only a fleeting relief. It was as close to prayer as I ever came; it did more for me than prayer ever could.

Where Her Mind Is

by Sharon Louise Stephenson

Rebecca and Amber are confronting a Bengal tiger. She watches from her seat on the golden oak floor, many square feet of comfortable living room awash in summer light; they stand silent as jurors, even the tiger. Rebecca is closer, blonde braid down her back, one arched hand reaching towards the cat's closed jaws, calming the beast. Amber's torso is tilted forward; it is awkward but her balance holds.

Later, Hugh will say, "Momma, don't put anyone away." She and her son Hugh and daughter Anna relocate all the Playmobil, the people, animals, huts, houses, even the bushes. Rebecca will be moved to higher ground, the coffee table. Amber too finds a safe perch, scooped from the scene by her human hand, a mother's hand, and smoothly lifted to a three–legged side table topped with copper. All must remain downstairs until play resumes.

They are ambitious, the sun is increasing, and she will drive Hugh and Anna in an outdated minivan to the swim and tennis club. Tomorrow Rebecca and Amber, her two Playmobil personas, will again be challenged. These plastic 7.6 cm women, toys to some, are extensions of her. Lightweight but hard as stone, they are lifted and lowered from tiger's side to police car to an elephant in labor. They are welcome everywhere. They offend no one. When she, their mother, becomes Rebecca and Amber, there is no discord, no argument. Rebecca and Amber are eternally grateful when Anna's Playmobil persona Daniel presents them with a Playmobil hamster or peacock. Rebecca and Amber are honestly interested in hearing about the conspiracy being hatched by the Playmobil 'bad guys' as told through Hugh's policemen personas, more often than not also named Hugh. The universe has simple rules. A Playmobil figure, once positioned, does not move.

All summer has been like this, the indoors heavy with air conditioning and yellow sun pouring through the windows, the sweet, humble puppy snuffling their Playmobil scenery, toppling a precise arrangement and exiled to the plump cushions of the couch. When the indoors are not enough, play expands onto lakes, beaches, rocks and lawn. It is a season of injury, a spider bite in the ear, staples in the scalp, mosquito bitten limbs, sunscreen tight on unwashed skin.

As the Playmobil is shuttled off to corners and tabletops, her reality divides and her mind moves to work: to edits of a journal article, to an overdue annual review of the electronics technician. Years ago these thoughts would have come uninvited and soured the afternoon; her speech would have become rapid and irritated, her movements impatient. The children, intuitive always, would have responded with panic.

But age has its gifts. Today she can call up the stressful reality of work and hold it at arm's length. She can rotate her thoughts with a slow, steady pace, appraising. Her children, intuitive always, now gently cup small toys with small hands. Her children, intuitive always, now quietly walk with bare, small feet on the golden floor.

30

While they are at the pool, she will silently organize to–do lists with her backside sprawling on a slatted lounge chair. Her eyes behind sunglasses frequently locate her Hugh, her Anna in the cold, clear pool water. She has little trust in lifeguards. They are young and inexperienced.

While the slats of the chair leave imprints on her backside, she will entertain other mothers in flip flops and coverups, and in one case, a breathtaking bikini. Each is not so young as to believe all pool eyes are on her and not so old as to have trouble controlling her hips and knees as she lowers onto an adjoining lounge chair. Behind their own large sunglasses, earnest faces talk of what they are reading and what they could be reading, texting Hilary Mantel and Chimamanda Ngozi Adichie to themselves for future reference, shading their cell phones from the sun with tilted torsos, legs thrown wide like little girls. Later their voices lower for worry–talk about the children. One child is too thin, one too heavy, one too slow to read, another has too few friends. She listens, she responds, she looks fully engaged with the other mothers.

But looks can deceive. She feels she is the only one aware of the perfection of these days, this life. She marvels at the small wind interrupting the afternoon heat. Clouds in stately towers, a thousand whites and greys. Unspoiled blue sky promising a secure heaven. While she listens, while she responds, she holds in her mind a reality where she is silent and swift, where she can leap from her chaise and with bare, tan feet stomp the earth, rocket into the atmosphere, a straight arrow, unimpeded by gravity.

31

Steps for My Uncle

by Layla Blackwell

I have one lasting memory of a task that most people do every day. A basic skill they take for granted. I was walking. I was five because I remember the shoes I was wearing that day: Doc Marten lace–ups with multi–coloured laces shining, like new, purchased for my first days at school.

My favourite possession was a white and navy, silver cross dolls pram with matching handmade accessories. I couldn't have been prouder to take it out and clean it on sunny days. Not that it really needed it, my pram had only ever gone as far as my back garden. The wheels had kept their original white and the body was unscratched, despite being in my care for years. That day, however, I wanted to take it on a journey.

I'd seen a million mothers pass my driveway with their prams and proud smiles. I wanted to know what that was like.

"Mum, can I go for a walk to see Uncle Steven? Can I take the pram?"

My mother looked at me then, a hint of sadness in her eyes. "It's pretty far darling, are you sure you want to go?"

I looked down at my feet and knew what she meant. It was

pretty far for someone like me.

"Yeah I know, but I want to try."

To get to my Uncle's house, you walked all the way along my street and around the corner. Walked up the little hill, then crossed a busy road. My sister is five years older than me and I had seen her take this journey a few times and when she returned she wasn't even out of breath. But for me, it was like attempting the English Channel without practising in a swimming pool first. Through the open window, I heard my mother as she picked up the phone and dialled my Uncle's number. Probably praying under her breath that he was working. But he picked up.

I settled my doll into her pram and tucked the blankets around her. Then I had to be helped into my splints. They're plastic moulds of the back of your leg that hold the foot in the correct position when weight is applied. The foot and leg are then held in the splint by Velcro straps, to stop your muscles from twisting. Pressure points formed on my ankle, the back of my heel and any other part of the foot that rubbed on it. Not to mention it sometimes stopped the circulation. They made my legs cold but it was still less painful than my feet twisting.

That done, Mum helped me into my shoes. Only then was I ready to stand. I had to do that before I could even attempt the steps needed for the trip.

The plan was for my mother to walk at my side. If I got too tired then my knees buckled.

"You're sure you want to do this?"

I nodded.

My mind was made up.

33

I was now just tall enough to push the pram. As my Mum waited for me to get my footing, I was pleased to have grown so much. My parents had also made sure the pram could withstand me leaning on it with a fair bit of weight, paying extra for the stronger frame. It also had brakes.

My mother stepped back and I took my first step.

Another step, followed by the next and the next. I thought about each step before I put one foot in front of the other. I kept my eyes on my doll as I walked. I couldn't let myself think about the pain because I would give in. Nothing I do is truly pain free, it means I'm living, in a way. A quarter of the way there, I ignored the pain in my knee. Half way there, and there was a pain in my hip.

"Are you okay?" my mother asked.

I couldn't answer. I bit my lip and simply continued. But after another three steps, I stopped and tried to catch my breath. I leaned as hard as I could on the handle of the pram.

"I can do it, Mum."

Mum said nothing.

When I was ready to push the boundaries again, I took another step. There's a wee trick I learned from my many years of physiotherapy. When you don't think you can go any further, aim for just one more step and continue. But my pride flickered like a candle against my pain. After a few more steps I surrendered.

My Mother knelt in front of me and wiped the sweat from my brow with her sleeve.

"You've done really well, darling. It's much further than I thought you'd get but I think you're tired."

I couldn't argue any more, the fight had left me. I flopped into my mother's open arms and looked over her shoulder. All I could see was the pavement, too tired now to even lift my head. And as my Mother carried me the rest of the way, I watched the surfaces beneath me change.

Notebooks

by Gessy Alvarez

Mother's notebooks contained sentences written in Spanish and then translated into English. She came to this country on a student visa, enrolled at the American Language Center. She wanted to be a secretary.

She blamed her brownness for her lack of prospects back home. In Ecuador the help wanted ads required secretaries to be young, white, and pretty. She kept her high school graduation picture in her wallet. She wore a white cap and gown. Her brown hands in white gloves. Mother never applied for a job in Ecuador.

When my grandmother moved to New York, she forged Mother's signature on a student visa application and lent her unmarried daughter money for a plane ticket.

Mother dropped out of the American Language Center after one semester when my grandmother asked for her money back, landed her first factory job in the garment district. For eight years, she sewed buttons on vinyl trench–coats.

The notebooks from that one semester were stored in a pillowcase. She liked to show me her notebooks, said it proved she was a good student.

Multi–colored drawings of circuit boards adorned Father's notebooks. He was a mechanic in the army. His superiors called him *Técnico* because he liked to fix short–wave radios.

When he arrived in New York from the Dominican Republic, he enrolled in a technical school to study air conditioning and refrigeration repair. The school was in Paterson, New Jersey, an hour bus ride away from the George Washington Bus Terminal in Washington Heights. His teachers and classmates were either Dominican or Puerto Rican. He never learned English. In six months, he earned a certificate. It was his only graduation.

Father had a school loan to pay off. He took the best job he could find. He pressed pants at a factory then later worked as a building porter in the Bronx.

After dinner, he always had somewhere to go. If I was lucky, he would let me tag along. Sometimes he'd catch me sprawled on the linoleum floor tracing and memorizing his old circuit drawings. He said his notebooks reminded him of time lost.

Enough

by Cinda Gibbon

I wasn't a fan of reality. My childhood was tense; my dad, a college professor and business owner, was a batterer. Reality meant yelling and backhanders. I preferred my books, and while I read, I never heard when called. The habit provoked my Dad. He referred to me as "Unconscious," as if it was my nickname, even inventing a new punishment, "The Door Knocker." If I hadn't stopped reading by the time he arrived, he knocked on my head with two knuckles as if my head were a front door. It was only delivered once because from then on I was on my feet before I saw his mismatched eyes – one blue, one green. Our relationship improved when I was an adult, because we both adored my son.

Tristan was born in Seattle in October 1984 on an evening when the sunset dripped cotton ball clouds of peach gilt against a lavender sky. My mom had come out to be with me for the birth, and all three of us flew out of Seattle a week later on a red–eye to Pittsburgh. We arrived at dawn, sleepless and stained by condiments and five kinds of body fluids. I was exchanging a failed marriage for single motherhood in my parents' home. I wasn't sure which was worse.

Tristan was social with a sunny disposition; he rarely cried. Woke no one but me through the night, smiled early and often, and easily burst into peals of giggles and outright baby guffaws. The longer he laughed the louder we laughed too. "Boy–joy" was better shared; my single motherhood wasn't singular.

Tristan and I moved to our own place—only a block away—when he was a year old. My mom cared for him while I took classes for my teaching certification. While I was in class, Dad started taking Tristan on outings: to the playground near our homes, to see his mother in the nursing home, or on his own errands.

I didn't mind initially. I was charmed when Tristan begged me to swing him at the playground. When I visited my grandma at the nursing home, I was proud – everyone knew his name. Tristan ran ahead to greet them and some details clicked in place. Tristan knew more than their names, he knew where they stashed their sweets. Sleuthing revealed that Tristan ate treats every day and had a stash of toys at my parents' larger than a dragon's hoard. Dad followed the letter not the spirit of my rules. If I said no candy, Tristan got a milkshake. If I said no guns, Dad bought plastic swords—27 of them! By the time I was offered two teaching positions in 1987, Tristan was pitching temper fits. I was relieved when the one furthest away offered first. Dad would be confined to weekend visits and I would have a chance to undo the emerging brat. I married Tom in 1989 and that too slowed down the visits. Shortly after we married, my sister had a boy; Dad spoiled him instead.

My dad died the Sunday after Easter, 1999, of mesothelioma, cancer usually caused by exposure to asbestos. Tiny inoperable tumors grow in the lining that protects the organs in the chest. Most sufferers die after three months of the diagnosis, but my dad lasted nearly three years. For Easter, Mom threw a huge party and my Dad was more jovial than I'd seen him in years. He usually hated my Mom's parties, but that day, he was fun.

The next Sunday he died. I almost did not go to visit. Tristan had plans and I had grading. I called, but Mom quavered, "He's been waiting for you." Me? It was Tristan he wanted, so I had Tris write him a letter and I went. Grumbling.

A hospital bed had been delivered, but he wouldn't lie in it. My mom whispered, "He calls it "The Coffin," but he hasn't slept in days. See if you can get him in it."

The hospice nurse arrived, and after her, my aunt, Dad's beloved sister, "Peaches." Mom took the nurse past the bed into the kitchen for paperwork and somehow Aunt Peaches convinced Dad to get in the bed. It took three of us: me, my sister, Cheri, and my aunt, but we made it. As he settled, he made a loud and ragged intake of air that sounded like the breath between sobs.

Mom was talking to the nurse in what we called her "Telephone Voice," so obviously she thought she was required to entertain the nurse. Cheri and Peaches took seats at the foot of the bed. Seeing no other role for myself, I perched at Dad's right shoulder and attempted to console him. I read Tristan's letter aloud.

> Dear Pap,
> Sorry I didn't come today, but I will see
> you again. Mom told me the seriousness
> of your condition and I am real sorry. So
> I wanted to tell you that you are a great
> granddad. I always have fun with you.
> I love you.
> Your grandson,
> Tristan

I only made it to the second line, I couldn't go on. The phrase "seriousness of your condition" sounded too formal. Until that

40

moment, I hadn't thought about how Tris would cope. Oh, Tristan … ! Dad …

I drove a turnaround every Sunday for two years to see my ever—more—emaciated father, except for three Sundays in January, 1999, when I was punishing him. I loved him but it was complicated by other emotions. Humiliation surely. Even when sick he scolded if I gained weight, wasn't wearing make—up, or hadn't dressed in a way pleasing to him. On January 3rd, 1999, it was guilt and fury. We watched golf and the food channel. Sometime before Tristan, then fourteen, and I left, he asked for a private talk. I was wary.

He led with this: "I have never forgiven you for going to the lawyer."

When I was sixteen, I pulled a knife on him.

On weeknights, if the restaurant he owned got busy, he called me to ferry supplies from the freezers and shelves in the garage. The phone had to be free. Because I was talking, he couldn't get through. Imagine that, a sixteen—year—old on the phone for more than a few minutes. I hung up when I heard his car. I repeated that I was sorry, but his head was down and menace was up − a one—two punch to my left shoulder and then a shove. I fell against the counter in front of the kitchen sink. He closed for the backhander. The knife drawer was to my left, and without thought, a butcher's knife appeared in my hands. I said nothing, but held his eyes − so terrifyingly different in his red face. None of us had ever fought back before. He hesitated, turned and tore the phone off the wall mount as he left.

The next week I went to the family lawyer to … I didn't know, I just wanted to make my dad stop hitting. The lawyer listened, and said he'd talk with my dad. I heard nothing more, but now Dad told me that the lawyer did indeed talk to him.

41

When he said he had never forgiven me, I heard it backwards—that he was asking me for forgiveness, but no, he was telling me to apologize. He said that telling the family business to anyone in a small town could have ruined his reputation or exempted him from financing; that he was dying, that soon I wouldn't have the chance. I morphed, dropping decades at a time, and it was a girl who cried, "Oh Daddy, I'm so sorry!"

Soon we left and the further I drove away the more furious I became. At the Bedford turnpike entrance ramp, the string of trucks followed as tightly as boxcars, I was forced to a full stop. Then I saw an opening and floored the accelerator. It wasn't an opening. The truck's horn blared and the rearview was filled with grille. Luckily the shoulder widened into a cindered rest area and I swerved to safety.

I punched the dashboard with the heel of my palm and Tristan popped up from the back seat. "Is something wrong with the car?"

"No."

Catching my mood, he said nothing and lay down. His body was longer than the width of the seat, bending at his hips and knees like a folding wooden yardstick. I had been driving this trip from my parents' home to my teaching job since he was two years old and still in a car seat. Sometimes the car felt like time suspended, like we spent his entire life in the car. His body shrinks or grows depending on my memories. I love Tristan so much, I couldn't be jealous of my father's love for him. Dad was different for Tris and that was enough. I sat there awhile, slowed my breathing, kicked myself for recklessness, and drove east.

Magic French Words

by Jonathan Slusher

I had a tight one–handed grip on the baby stroller. Two fingers from my other hand were wrapped inside the perfect miniature fist of a three year old. We rumbled over Pont Alexandre III early in the morning, just in time to watch a Seine barge ripple the mirror image of the old bridge. I stared as the barge sailed on. Would moments like this truly be something the kids and I would take with us forever, wherever we went? Was Paris really a moveable feast? I wanted to think so.

As we strolled through Jardin des Tuileries a long queue outside the Louvre came into focus. Thousands of people were packed tightly into a nightmarish snake that zigzagged well past the rope turnstiles. The wait would have been at least an hour. Stuck in an anxious multilingual gaggle of frayed nerves and boredom, Sophie would have to go potty, and Lukas never lasted long once the stroller stopped rolling. We turned a corner and called it quits.

Plan B was set to include ice cream, television, air conditioning, and naptimes for all three of us. However, as we rumbled along Rue de Rivoli a museum side entrance appeared. I read the sign slowly and plucked out a few words.

Groupes d'adultes et les groupes de jeunes encadrés par des adultes.

Did an expatriate American stay—at—home daddy with two small kids and a stroller constitute a tour group? Probably not, but it was worth a shot. I stood waiting for the guard to finish talking with his snappily—dressed colleague before giving my debutant level French all that it had.

"Pardon, c'est possible pour nous?" I nodded towards the door.

The guard looked at the kids for a moment then responded with a rapid string of French words that I couldn't pull apart.

"Nondésoléec'estimpossibleicimonsieur."

I thought I got the drift of it. *Sorry pal.* But then he smiled at my daughter. "Suis—moi madame," he said and waved his arm.

I didn't know what that meant. Was he asking us to follow him? He spun around so quickly I wasn't sure. I followed him, bumping the stroller across the cobblestones through swaying groups of wandering tourists. Lukas bounced wildly as we stepped on the gas. Sophie held on tight to my hand, her feet barely touching the ground. The guard never once turned around and he walked much too fast. He should have looked back to make sure we were still behind him. Had he really asked us to follow him? Was it a misunderstanding? Maybe it was a joke on me and he was trying to lose us! I spotted his navy hat in the crowd then lost it again.

Suddenly all of the things everyone ever said about the rudeness of the French were proving to be very real. Some of my friends and friends of those friends had warned my wife and me not to move here. I was a *stupide* American. Frustrated yet determined, I picked up the pace and tried hard to keep the guard's hat in sight. I bit my bottom lip. What a jerk! *The French*, they really did hate us. Nothing like this would ever happen in the United

44

States. My homeland was better organized and much less confusing. Americans looked out for each other. I couldn't think of any specific examples, but it was a fact that everyone knew. I was sure that it was. Things were definitely different there, especially when you had kids with you.

We'd only been living abroad for two months and already I was longing to be back in familiar territory. In the States I could get around without thinking too hard. George W. was halfway into his second presidential term. U.S.A., U.S.A., it was a time when the rest of the world was either with us or against us. And many felt that France was definitely against us. But I *had* to see things for myself. My secret unofficial American ambassador plans for success included keeping an open mind and learning the French language. I wanted to broaden my horizons, correct misconceptions, and experience a new culture, spending my days behind the stroller, wandering through the City of Light. Like a vacation, I would chat fluently with the locals and smoke an occasional Gauloises at the brasserie. Well, that was my plan.

Driving in the city was a nightmare. Bikes, buses, and pedestrians were everywhere and so many rules were ignored, I didn't know which ones to follow. Even walking with the kids could be scary. *Vous traversée avec deux côte. Priorité a droit.* Only a few days before, I'd almost been run down by a Smart Car.

Sophie missed her best friend from Connecticut. My wife was traveling a lot for her new job. French telemarketers, our landlord, my daughter's new school, train ticket machines, and forms for the Préfecture des Yvelines. I craved *chasson aux pommes*, but couldn't pronounce the pastry correctly. At the boulangerie I often had to settle for a plain baguette.

I was annoyed at myself for whining so much. But the French really *didn't* welcome foreigners. My solace would be informing friends and family of the blasphemies we would endure.

45

I sighed and shook my head. And then saw where we were: at the very front of the long line. The guard unfastened a brass hook, lifted up the rope, and guided Sophie through with a gentle hand on her back. The smirk on his face hinted at things I couldn't identify in my confusion. I pushed the stroller into the glass elevator then turned around.

"Bonne journée Monsieur," the guard said, smiling as if I was someone who mattered.

The doors closed and we descended, as other tourists turned up their hands, stared, and muttered incredulously.

"Merci," I mumbled, five seconds too late.

Alone in a glass elevator inside a glass pyramid, my daughter beamed up at me. I had forgotten I was still holding her small hand. Tiny ten-month-old chortles may have even risen up out of the stroller. I can't say for sure. And I don't remember how long we lasted in the museum, either, but it doesn't matter. For one day the kids and I were Musée du Louvre VIPs.

Things Left Behind

by Claire Ibarra

She had announced that she was leaving, to both of us, separately. She told my father with promises of coming back one day. To me, it was announced after I was caught cutting class. I lounged with my friends on the couch, gorging on chocolate kisses dipped in peanut butter, while watching an episode of *All My Children*. My mother said, "Come with me, we need to talk."

I slouched on the edge of the bed, thinking I was busted for skipping out of school. The banter and laughter of my friends came through the door, while she gazed at me. Her eyes softened with sympathy, but she didn't smile. I can't remember our conversation, except for her repeated assurance. "It's all for the best," she said. "It's all for the best."

I remember my three friends hugging me, as they tried to comfort me afterward. I've never cried easily, but I figured it was expected, so my tears that day were mostly for the benefit of my friends. I was thirteen, fiercely independent, and already used to the ups and downs of my parents' marriage.

It had happened before when I was seven. There was yelling and screaming in the driveway. My dad, angry and protective, carried

47

me into the house. I watched from behind the screen door. My mom climbed into a red jeep and drove away with another man. Confused by her sudden departure, I cried, while tugging at the frayed mesh on the screen door.

My father took me on a long camping trip to Big Sur. Our flee to the wilderness of the redwoods was meant to distract me and soothe his pain. And since my dad didn't tell my mom where we were going, it also served to punish her.

Yet, my mother's announcement that she was leaving us again was not the defining moment.

It came later…

It came after she moved out the last of her things, and her closet and bathroom were left bare of her lacy vintage clothes, her jewelry, and her musky floral scent.

It came after my father and I grew accustomed to a routine without her. I did my own laundry and walked to school. I spent as much time as I could at friends' homes. I ate meals at other families' tables or pizza out of the box. My father and I drifted through the house like spirits lingering after an untimely death. We were bewildered, lost and detached.

It came one evening as I crept through the house. Wandering from my bedroom into the dimly–lit kitchen, I stood for a few moments. The hum of the refrigerator was the only sign of life. Then my dad walked in. I couldn't recall ever standing there together before—it seemed new and strange.

"So, what shall we have for dinner?" Dad said, feigning cheer. He walked over to the refrigerator and opened it with wide eyes, as if a home–cooked meal would appear before him by magic. I stood beside him, and we stared at the expired carton of milk and the rotten iceberg lettuce. The refrigerator was a white cavern, barren and cold, and smelled spoiled and moldy.

The refrigerator was a reflection of our lives.

I froze. I watched my dad's shoulders fall and slouch. His head hung low and his eyes were downcast. He sobbed, and putting his arms around me, hugged me close, desperate and grasping for life.

I had caught a glimpse of my parents' flaws at seven years old, when I watched my mother drive away in that jeep with another man. I knew she was only thinking of herself, when she should have been thinking of her family, and me, her only child.

I began to understand my dad's avoidance and despondency, while watching him play his classical guitar surrounded by redwoods during our extended vacation at Big Sur. It was easier to escape to his music and the forest than face a home and life without her.

While he strummed flamenco at the skirt of the forest, I jumped off boulders and twirled myself around and around, like Wonder Woman. If I was like Wonder Woman, then wasn't my father able to be a super hero, too? I wanted to feel secure and safe. I wanted to know he could get her back.

Now at thirteen years old, my dad's vulnerability frightened me. As I stood in the middle of my family's cold and empty kitchen, I took a step back and told myself, "You have to take care of yourself."

§

My father came to visit a few weeks ago. We worked in the kitchen together, beside my husband and daughters. My father sautéed mushrooms in butter and wine. My husband rinsed clams, mussels and shrimp for paella. My daughters debated the

49

health risks of GM foods. I chopped garlic. We drank wine, my teenage girls stealing sips, and we listened to Santana. The sounds of electric guitar and conversation filled the room.

"Can you get out the cilantro?" my husband asked. He then made a joke to my dad about clams, their odor and uncanny resemblance, as he peered inside a shell.

I opened the refrigerator, filled with fruits and vegetables and containers of leftovers. The milk carton would not expire for two more weeks and the romaine lettuce was green and fresh. I held the cilantro to my nose and breathed in the sweet scent. Shutting the door, I closed my eyes. Then I rinsed the cilantro, placed it on the wood block, and began chopping the fine leaves.

friends

Malcolmina XOX

by Rebecca Chekouras

This morning I am up and outside early waiting for a neighbor because we have a date to go to the Laney College flea market—the great, traveling souk that comes to Oakland every Sunday with music blaring, corn and tamales roasting, piles of junk, and an entire department store complete with cooking demonstrations laid flat on burning asphalt. I am 10 minutes into a large coffee that has me shaking like a bobble–head Chihuahua in the rear window of a Chevy. But my friend is oblivious because he is putting his makeup on and that takes time as any diva can tell you. I don't mind waiting for him to become her. It's going to be a great day so it is odd that I should be musing on the nature of revenge.

Being an outcast in a society that imagines itself progressive is a wound of a thousand daily insults; never a direct kill. The wound builds just as a desire for revenge does. Until a person has experienced the punishing humiliation of having their basic human dignity put to a popular vote, which is the very essence of Prop 8 in California, they can never understand the rage that I have tamed every day. It is hidden in the posture I assume when I say I am okay to reassure the straight people who are my friends. I am not okay. I am anything but okay and thus I am thinking about revenge and how I came to understand the impulse as wrong—not for moral reasons or the terrible brickbat of Christian love, but for self–preservation.

What is the revenge of those without power? Do the powerless exact only a puny, unseen, unfelt revenge and, if so, is that really revenge? Isn't the essential nature of revenge that it is felt by its target; felt as deeply as the hurt it is intended to remedy? When I was a child, I spent hours—no, years—plotting revenge against an older brother who baited me like a caged bear. He pestered, poked, bullied, and hit until I cried in helpless rage. He stole from me, broke my favorite toys, lied to our parents blaming me for trouble he caused and they believed him. I hated him so thoroughly, I wished he were dead. That is the revenge of an eight–year–old with a terrible secret.

I first understood that the world would not be welcoming to me when I was in middle school—that great sorting bin. Children sense the stakes are high and the ethos of elementary school— sharing and mutual respect—give way to a fierce and ruthless social jockeying. When boys bullied each other with *homo* and *queer*, words I didn't know, I was stunned that these taunts could knock a rival down more surely than a fist.

One small freedom we in my little Catholic school had was the right to get up at any time to consult the big dictionary at the front of the classroom. It was, in fact, considered the mark of a dedicated young mind. Thus entitled, I walked from my seat at the back of the room all the way to the front and began to page through the dictionary to find out why those words had such power to devastate. In that moment, as I read what a homo was, my life disintegrated. There, in front of my entire class, I learned I was a pariah, someone to be made fun of, and fair game to every bully or worse. I could barely turn around and face my known, lost world or get back to my seat without fainting. I understood then that I would serve a life sentence for a crime I did not commit.

As I grew older, I simply gave up, choosing to bide my time under the radar as much as possible until I could break free and escape my family and religion. Ultimately, it was a good strategy. Once I left home I never looked back but kept moving forward into some unknown life that would be, whatever else it might have to offer, better. After an entire decade of distilling in the crucible of university, I emerged in Chicago where I stood on the train platform in full-on corporate drag every morning, commuting to a corner office so high up that I could look down on the traffic helicopters. I ran an international research business while my bullying brother became an alcoholic who couldn't hold a job. Revenge, simmering so long on the back burner, was finally done. What I didn't know then was that my desire for revenge, against my brother, Catholicism, a nation of bigots, had dangerously burned the pan that cooked it—me.

The LGBT people of my generation have had to hide a huge part of our natural selves just to get by in a world that does not want us. I was 40 years old before I could talk to co-workers about my whole, integrated life without fearing the loss of my job. In more than a dozen U.S. states, I could still be fired. I know now that my generation has paid dearly for being so marginalized. It is in the pit of ever-anger we carry in our stomachs. And, for me, it became a desire for revenge I could barely conceal.

It took a long time for me to grow weary of a business career based mainly on being what my brother couldn't—successful— and eventually, I walked out of my corner office to do work that meant something to me. I forgot about revenge but persisted in a hugely damaging need to be right all the time until the day my brother settled the barrel of a shotgun between his teeth and pulled the trigger. Then my seething righteousness was painfully evident to me and hollow. It is no longer possible for me to savor a win when someone else loses so badly. I lost the need for revenge; I no longer needed to be right. I wanted to be whole.

This morning is the eighth anniversary of my brother's suicide. As Malcolmina flounces to the curb to embrace me with a dozen kisses and escort me up the avenue, it is obvious that gay people are lovers not fighters and therein lies both our greatest strength and most debilitating weakness—we have been slow to demand our rights. Like the unwanted girl children in parts of Asia, we have acclimated to gruel while our fat brothers gorge; taking anything they want from a table where there is no seat for us. Instead, we are left sitting in the dirt with sticks and rocks. Shall we demand revenge or shall we be creative?

Using an ancient alchemy, gay people have ground those rocks against the stone of prejudice and manufactured glitter and eye shadow. We have taken our sticks and pounded them down on packed earth to create the pulsing beat of disco and house. We have taken the vile manure of hatred and created a garden—a culture focused on sensuality and pleasure pulled from the thin air of repression. Any scorn inflicted by the straight majority comes back to them, presto change–o, as something they cannot live without: hair styles, couture, beats, and home décor.

Swinging down the street with my friend Malcolmina XOX, a black drag queen the size of a city bus, I am buoyed by love for this royal woman who takes not one ounce of shit from anyone. Pink hair flouncing with each step, her yellow skirt blowing in the breezy summer morning, her polka dot handbag swinging like a metronome, she is a monarch butterfly. "I keeps it real," she tells me and it is true.

The Rose

by Diana J. Wynne

The woman who needs to create works of art is born with a kind of psychic tension in her which drives her unmercifully to find a way to balance, to make herself whole. Every human has the need. In the artist it is mandatory. Unable to fulfill it, he goes mad. But when the artist is a woman she fulfills it at the expense of herself as a woman.
– May Sarton

When other women her age were raising children, Jay DeFeo was painting *The Rose*. The most important painter of the Beat generation, DeFeo devoted more than seven years to this singular work of art.

Calling it a painting is misleading. *The Rose* is the size of a double bed, or a small tomb. I first saw it in Bruce Conner's film *The White Rose*, which documents the removal of *The Rose* from DeFeo's San Francisco apartment. It took up a whole wall of her Victorian. They had to remove it with a forklift, so the paint—a ton in all—would not crumble. I finally saw *The Rose* in person a few years ago and found myself hypnotized. It's a delicate piece despite its mass, a giant gray star. Rays of white light radiate out from the center in thick, harsh diagonal lines. You find yourself drawn right to its center.

DeFeo was already famous when she began to work on it at 29. During the 60s, *The Rose* was known mostly by reputation, not because anyone had actually seen it. Day after day, DeFeo painted layer upon layer of white lead paint. Almost a foot deep, it looked more like plaster than oil paint. After it was moved in 1965, not yet finished, it was nearly impossible to display because it had already begun to crumble.

I imagine Jay DeFeo in her studio, sitting on her paint—covered stool, relentlessly perfecting brush strokes, scraping away white paint and reapplying. Wanting to move on to something new, unable to stop. Waking up for breakfast and seeing it. Having friends like Allen Ginsberg and Bruce Conner jokingly ask what she was working on, for seven years. Identifying with one piece of art so strongly she often did not leave her flat for days on end. (Had she gone mad?)

I understand this, even though I'm not a famous painter or poet. Despite years of searching, I've never managed to join a salon of up—and—coming artists.

When I first moved to San Francisco, I lived in North Beach with two students at the Art Institute. They worked on experimental films while I worked downtown at McKinsey & Company, preparing management consulting reports for Wells Fargo and Apple. Ingrid and Jennifer would knock on my door late on a Tuesday night.

"We're going to record sound in the Marina Safeway. Wanna come?" We usually ended up at the House of Pancakes on Lombard Street at 2 am. It was not quite like being Kerouac and Ginsberg and Jay DeFeo. I was not quite James Joyce or Djuna Barnes, exiled in Paris.

Jennifer designed an alternative projection piece for one class. Like me, she came from the East Coast and often marveled at the constancy of weather in California. The piece was called *Absence of Seasons*.

She planned to project a film loop of blue sky, with only a cloud or two rolling in, onto a giant screen suspended over the heads of the audience. We would hear sound effects—wind, rain, sleet—but see only blue sky. It was a brilliant concept.

Every night as I came up the stairs in my Casual Corner blazer, fresh from photocopying bar charts on an impending reorg, we'd have these discussions. "What do *you* think?" she'd ask. "Should I stay in school or go back to Atlanta?" There was a subtext to this question. *Should I stay here and be a weird artist, and flirt with strange men, or should I go back to the safety of my middle-class parents and get married?*

It was an interesting conversation, at least the first ten or twenty times. I never failed to get sucked in, always taking the side of the artist's life in San Francisco, the one I was not quite living.

Jennifer spent weeks constructing the projection screen. She decided to sew shower curtains together, 16 x 16 shower curtains. We didn't have a sewing machine, so every time anyone came over, they would be enlisted, sitting on the edge of the bed or cross-legged on the floor sewing shower curtains, a Bohemian sewing bee.

The big night finally came, and I went to class after work. Jennifer had strung the curtains up, ten feet above our heads. She had the rain and dirt and sound effects all ready. But she'd failed to account for the final image size, because the projector was too close to the "screen." We stood under this white plastic tent and a small square of blue sky appeared above us. She valiantly poured water and dirt from on high. Some of it trickled down through the seams, leaving us damp and a little muddy down

59

below. Of course, at the time, the most creative thing I was doing was putting cardboard frames onto transparencies and binding reports at midnight.

I don't know if you can be a great artist without being possessed by your work. Surrounded by it, living and breathing shower curtains or mallard ducks, or whatever it is that drives you. It's not really the devotion that troubles me, it's the lack of boundaries. What if I lose track of that distinction but don't have the talent?

The Rose destroyed Jay DeFeo's life. No one likes to say this. They say she was blocked for years, and sometimes they write about how *The Rose* was crumbling in storage in a basement at the San Francisco Art Institute.

What they do not say is that as a result of working in such close quarters, DeFeo developed lead poisoning. She lost her hair. Her teeth fell out. Although she sketched and painted, and taught for a time at Mills College, she died of cancer at 60.

Since then *The Rose* has been rescued by the Whitney Museum. Exhibits devoted to DeFeo tour the country, and her place among 20th-century artists finally feels secure. Few of these retrospectives mention her illness except as a footnote.

Jay DeFeo never blamed *The Rose* for ruining her life. Not the way I do. She was going to keep painting, even if it killed her or drove her mad. Meanwhile I struggle to produce a great work of art and have a real life, determined to define myself in an absence of children, or tragedy.

Indelible Impression

by Mark Rosenblum

I noticed them when she removed her coat. I tried not to stare, but seeing in person what I had only read and heard about secondhand, was too tantalizing to ignore.

§

When I was an acne–faced teen, a high school friend, Mike, was in the hospital for gall bladder surgery. I remember driving my first car, a '68 Ford Galaxy 500 to the hospital. I maneuvered it through the parking lot like a whale trying to avoid hitting the miniature castle in a goldfish bowl. And in true teenage fashion, I had all the windows down while the radio blared The Bee Gees, *Stayin' Alive*, sharing their falsettos with those around me.

On my way to Mike's room, I spotted a bedpan on a cart. I walked into his room with it and told him I had found his report card outside. He smiled, then told me to screw myself.

I leaned back in a worn visitor's chair that would've been happy to call the Salvation Army home. My friend ate Jell–O from a lunch tray as we bullshitted about nothing.

A cute nurse came in and checked his chart. When she left I asked him if she was going to shave him before surgery. He said, "I can only hope."

I was there for about an hour when a head poked into the room. It was a neighbor from Mike's apartment building. I told Mike I should get going, but he told me to stay and meet his neighbors, David and his mother Eva. After a nurse provided extra chairs, we sat around and kept our friend company.

While David and I spent the time ribbing Mike, Eva was the proper mom. She asked about the surgery, how Mike was feeling and fluffed up his pillow.

About five minutes into our discussion of hospital food and its unsavory reputation (of which Mike was quick to point out the exception being Jell–O), Eva took off her coat and draped it over her chair. That's when I noticed the numbers tattooed on her arm.

Six million killed because of a religion, my religion. From history classes I had learned the twisted propaganda of Aryan supremacy, foreign enemies and Jewish subversion. From school documentaries I had seen skeletal bodies shoveled by bulldozers into mass graves. From novels and films I had learned of starvation, experiments, forced labor and executions. But now, for the first time, I saw the reality of hate embedded in another human being. I knew the tattoo on her arm once identified her as a prisoner, and now marked her as a survivor.

I tried not to stare, but she caught my gaze. "I am an Auschwitz survivor," she said. The words spoken without pity or pride.

"I'm Jewish too," I told her. It seemed like the right thing to say at the moment, a fellow Jew being sympathetic, but it came out trite. As if my lineage could bandage the wounds of the holocaust.

"Did you lose any of your family?" she asked.

No," I said. "From what I know, they emigrated many years before the Nazis came to power."

"I was about the same age as the three of you when our family was rounded up," she said. "I was separated from my parents, and I never saw them again."

"We've seen documentaries in school about the camps," said Mike, who was not Jewish.

I nodded in agreement.

Eva said, "It is good that schools do such things. Those who forget the past are condemned to repeat it."

"Do you remember a lot of what happened back then?" I asked.

She looked straight into my eyes and said, "Everything, like it was yesterday."

I had recently seen the movie *The Boys from Brazil*, about Dr. Mengele, the physician who performed experiments on prisoners in Auschwitz.

"Did you ever see Dr Mengele?" I asked.

She turned away and stared out the window. For a moment, I thought maybe I shouldn't have asked, but then she said, "He was called the Angel of Death."

She turned back toward me and continued, "Every few days, a group of women would be taken from our barracks and only

63

some would return. One morning, six girls were led outside by two guards and were told to form a line. I was one of them. One of the guards told us to remove our clothing. We stood in the middle of the camp, naked. Six bald women with bones pushed up against pale skin. I felt nothing. Vanity and pride had lost all meaning. I no longer considered myself a woman, or for that matter, a human being. A man came out of the medical barracks. He came toward us accompanied by a large German Shepherd on a leash. The dog sniffed around our bare legs, his nose was wet and cold. The man slowly walked around the six of us. He studied our bodies, looked at our faces, and stared into our eyes. He spoke to the guard, and pointed out two of the girls. The guard separated them from our group and told the four of us remaining to dress, then led us to our quarters. I looked back for a moment and watched the guard escort the two girls to the medical barracks. The man walked casually behind them, like he was on a stroll, taking his dog for a walk in a park. This was Dr. Mengele."

§

When I drove back from the hospital I turned the radio off. At a stop sign, I stared at the AM/FM dial numbers and watched as they morphed into the tattoo.

64

A Curious Fellow

by Shane Simmons

My mother stopped in her tracks and turned to me. "Don't walk like that, people will think you're... you're... gay."

It had been a quiet and uneventful stroll along the grey pavements of southeast London up until then. Making our way back home after visiting my sister for Sunday lunch, the streets were in fact quite empty.

And I wasn't quite certain how I should alter my steps to suit my mother's ideals.

§

My epilepsy medication made for another drowsy Monday morning. Walking through the school gates and taking a tentative scan, I straightened up and made my way through the group of boys taking up more than their fair share of the tarmac and kicking a football around.

"Get out of the way you poof!"

There were giggles from the others. Eyes forward, I pretended not to hear and carried on.

"You girl!"

It wasn't even 9 am and I wanted to go home and curl up in bed. The bell rang and the countdown to hometime began.

§

When we walked in, there was a distinct smell of stale moisture.

A family holiday. Crammed into two small and damp chalets with intense relations in the most mundane of long–dead English seaside towns, Clacton–upon–Sea.

"HE'S A POOF!"

I cringed as my brother made this proclamation to everyone in earshot. It's hard to sink down and disappear on a barstool. His eyes darted around our clan, looking for some sign of their agreement. But no one looked up from their greasy spoon chips.

"He likes ABBA!" he added.

He snorted, disappointed this evidence to back up his first statement was, again, mostly ignored.

I looked down at the soggy mess of chips, onion vinegar and ketchup. My stomach turned as I pushed the plate away.

My brother, following our father's 'waste not want not' declaration, grabbed the rejects closer, and jabbed his fork in. I wanted to thrust the plate whole into the gaping cavern he was so busy stuffing.

Back at the chalet I pulled the diary from my rucksack and crossed out another day. Six days to go.

§

"When we played football, we played real football," my father said. "No shin pads and we went right in for the legs, that's real tackling. Crack!" His well-worked hands gestured like a caveman snapping bones. "And when someone did that to you, well, they were in for it. Blood, broken ankles, we didn't mess about like these pansies."

I'd come downstairs to sit with my father, with no one else around, my mother upstairs, the house was at a rare quiet, except for the football on the television in the corner.

He sat back, a tired and wry smile on his face. As he made a stash of roll-up cigarettes for the next day, the dank fruity smell of tobacco filled the room with equal measures of repulse and allure. Roll, flick, lick, roll, flick, lick. They could've installed him in a cigarette factory.

"They need to have boxing in schools these days, it would make you into a man's man." He glanced at the TV, sat up straight with a jump and pointed his finger viciously at the screen.

"He's a queer fairy!"

My stomach turned over and I squirmed in my seat. Julian Clary was on the box. I wanted to giggle as he minced across in black sequin hot pants, throwing cheap double entendres in our direction, but as he became the focus of my father's sudden tirade I stopped myself from even cracking a smile.

§

Freeing myself of a rucksack filled with hefty textbooks, I sprinted up the stairs, closed the bedroom door and slipped on my battered headphones.

We had started swapping mix–tapes, each filled with visceral screams, grinding guitars and pounding drums that spun adrenaline through my veins until I could no longer control the excitement, my arms striking drums that weren't there, hands strumming guitars of thin air.

Lingering around after lunch, my musical education was complete before we'd even stepped in Mr Ryan's classroom. Our voices grew louder and our hand gestures wilder. "Nirvana? Grunge? That... that's all... that's just noisy 'stuff'! Isn't it...?" I said. When facing this one boy, my speech lost all coherence. My tongue tangled and words tumbled out in a freefalling mess.

As fresh snowfall floated down, I stuck my tongue out towards the sky and glimpsed him sparking a smile. My spine quivered. Goosebumps prickled my arms, and the flakes touched down, tasteless.

A snowball splattered against my chest. I could see the culprit, his smile turned mischievous. I scraped up and shaped my return shot. As he fled across the grass, I pulled my arm back to throw it in his direction, only to watch him slide on to his backside. He turned back to face our laughter, crimson–cheeked and yet still beaming. I let the ice melt through my fingers.

"COME DOWN NOW! You have to eat something!" I ignored the calls, slammed the door shut and pushed the bolt across. No distractions outside my room, not homework, school, neither family nor dinner could prise me away from the music, or the moment.

§

Avoiding each other's gaze, stealing glances as we turned corners and looked in shop windows, we wandered around London all day. Every second, I just wanted to touch him. Check he was there, feel him three-dimensional and breathing and real.

Later, "For goodness sakes, will the two of you just get it over and done with!" my lesbian friend demanded. Under the blaring cheesy-pop she sighed and disappeared into the crowd.

I'd never been inside a gay bar before.

Stood there, shoe-gazing, our sweaty, sticky palms met. He grasped my hand. I looked up at him, taller, broader than me. Each breath trembled through my body. I can't do this. I want to do this so much.

My free hand jumped over his shoulder. I tugged him, built like a brick shithouse, and my lips glued onto his. He tasted of bitter lager. I fingered the nape of his neck, exploring where the skin turned to freshly trimmed hair. I drew my hand around his face, stroking the sandpaper stubble on his cheek.

I pulled away. We stared at each other. Me not breathing.

I wouldn't have minded if he missed his coach back to Scotland, not in the slightest and yet we sprinted up the road.

I sank into the warmth of his torso, his girthy arms tight around me, hugging for far longer than two men usually do in a busy London coach station. I said, "I'll come up and see you, I promise."

Outside the entrance the part-time chaperone had caught up. My knees shook as I burst into tears. "Don't be such a poof!" she shouted. Her slur got my back up and I tried to glare at her but

69

laughed through hysterical gasps instead. Then sobbed. And cleared my eyes and blew my nose with a tissue or ten as we strolled back up Buckingham Palace Road.

They'd all known. For all those years they'd been right. And now I didn't care, not a jot. I had a date to keep with a man from Glasgow.

§

"Last night my girlfriend outed me on Facebook."

To have a new security guard at work who doesn't resemble death, scar–faced and microwave–heated, and has a cute smile, is a rarity. We'd been talking about music and film and books and found we both have tastes alternative to the Glasgow norm. And now this.

"I left my mobile in her reach when I went to the toilet and she posted, *I have to come clean guys, I'm gay*, on my wall."

I smirk.

He leans in to whisper, "I got a private message from one of my friends. It was him coming out, he asked me if I fancied going on a date with him! And he wasn't joking."

I snort.

"Don't laugh!" he shouts, "It was kinda confusing, you know!"

Walking into the staff room the next day, the guard sits scoffing chips and cheese.

I plonk myself down to get ready for work. "That looks healthy!"

He looks up, half–melted stringy cheddar dangling from his mouth. He licks it away with his tongue. "Erm, you're not gay, are you?"

Only there a day and he's already heard, stupid fucking gossips. "What makes you ask?" I grunt.

"Well, I just assumed you were... you know..."

"Normal?"

I watch him squirming on his chair.

"So, I'm not normal?" His chubby fingers rapping the table, I can't deny taking some sadistic pleasure in making him uncomfortable. I bite my lip trying not to laugh.

"I just didn't think you could be gay. Your taste in music and stuff, it's a bit deceiving isn't it?"

I inhale sharply through clamped teeth.

"Deceiving? So you reckon I'm a liar because I have *exceptionally* good taste in music?" He looks away and I notice a gulp in his throat. "Or how about this, seeing as I don't neatly fit your ideals of Kylie and musicals for the homos, that must make you somewhat less 'straight' ... right?"

His face glows red.

I stand up. "Don't worry mate, you're not really gay!" I say, patting him on the back as I walk past on my way to the kettle. "Just an ickle bit bi–curious perhaps."

71

foibles

Itch

by Joanna Delooze

I was imagining myself sliding. his pink. silk. tie. aside.

slowly.

Unbuttoning his razor crisp white shirt.

Running my hands, clinging closer than a diver's suit, up his milk chocolate chest and across shoulders that belonged to a linebacker

when he said–

smirking, ever so slightly–

"Mrs Delooze? I am sorry to laugh, but I've been an MS doctor for ten years now and I've never heard of this ..." He sucked his lips in and around his teeth hard, grinding them together in an effort not to laugh. In the end he hid behind his clipboard. But I could see his shoulders

earthquaking

"...anyways, it's quite *unusual*."

My nurse, and friend for the eight years since I was diagnosed, sat behind the desk to the left of me, busied herself with paperwork on her knee. Didn't look me in the eye.

She knew. She knew what I hadn't mentioned to him yet.

That I was sat there, knickerless under my skirt, while I poured out my distress to a visiting consultant who looked like a Ralph Lauren underwear model.

I had been expecting my regular doctor, a granddad only a few years from retirement.

The visiting doctor had a crisp Oxford accent to match his crisp white shirt.

I wondered if, underneath it, his chest was hairy, and squirmed on my seat.

"Erm... *most unusual.* How long have you been... *distressed* with this?"

I cringed, and looked at the floor. "Well over a month now, honestly it's unbearable."

§

"Call the bloody doctor tomorrow or I will," he threatened when I'd woken him up at 3 am, begging, again. For at least the fourth time this week.

After calling him at least twice during the previous work day.

After calling him almost *every day* in the last week.

76

"I can't take it, you have to come home. I can't concentrate on anything, my legs keep giving out when it hits, I can't think straight. I *need* you. *NOW*."

"Forget it. I am not coming home on my lunch break. Get in the shower, turn the sprayer on massage and sort yourself out. Stay in there all day if you like. I'm *knackered*, okay???"

§

There're things they tell you. And things they don't.

It's not malicious, I'm sure. Everyone's different. Symptoms, difficulties, progress of the disease.

It's very hard for a doctor to tell you which category you will come under, which particular crack in the sidewalk will open up and swallow you.

Some people go blind with it.

Some are in wheelchairs fairly early on and never get out again.

Some climb a mountain one month, and then need to be fed like a baby the next, their muscles and nerves giving them so much hell their body shuts down.

And me?

Well it varied. Almost blind in one eye for a few months; then miraculously fine upon waking one random morning.

Three months once when I looked like I had Bell's palsy. The left side of my face collapsed and hanging down like a Dali painting, my eye twitching so rapidly I had to wear sunglasses to hide it. Everyone thought I was winking at them.

77

Sometimes able to do aerobics for weeks at a time, because miraculously, I felt like myself again. But of course, I paid for it. One light class, competing with the grannies, thinking I was Wonder Woman and then needing to sleep all afternoon to recover.

Deadfromthewaistdown for almost six months when I was finally diagnosed. It was so bad then that the doctor made me shut my eyes while he rammed a tetanus needle up to its hilt in my thigh, testing my awareness.

It was so deep

So deep under my skin

Standing self–supported like a soldier

at attention on my thigh

and

I never

felt it going in.

But *this* was worse. Way worse. I was suffering.

SUF–FER–ING

With hypersensitive nerve endings on the surfaces of my skin. Usually that just meant that my legs looked like a Yeti because a razor blade felt like fingers of sharp knives filleting my calves as I shaved.

But MS likes to shake things up, keep you guessing, it likes to set up shop wherever the hell it pleases.

I had ditched my knickers, jeans and riding in cars whenever possible.

Poised on a rollercoaster's edge about to drop over the highest plunge... stalled. Engine rev, rev, revving...

that surging urging oooohhhhh...... leading leading leading...

And never stopping. Never resolving. Never going away.

The husband *was* knackered and sick of walking like he'd just climbed off a horse.

There're some parts of your body that don't take kindly to the Energizer Bunny and all his mates creating a warren and setting their phazers to zap mode.

"I believe I can give you something for that," he said crisply.

... right here on the desk? NOW? Yes... **Pleeeeease**. *please pleaseplease*

"The tablets usually take about 2 weeks to work fully but you should start to feel some reduction in sensation within about 3 days."

Tablets???

Damn.

Greetings from Havana

by Gloria Frym

When one is introduced to a person for the first time, one says, *Mucho gusto*, or *Un placer*, offering a handshake or a kiss.

When departing a new acquaintance, the same. If the conversation is warm and personal, the Cuban will kiss your right cheek upon departing and likely your left cheek as well.

When you see the person again, as a gesture of recognition among females, the Cuban woman will kiss your right cheek, then your left, then your right. Sometimes two men will semi-hug while shaking right hands.

Also when seeing the person again, one must inquire, *¿Como te vas?* or *¿Como has sido?* or make a statement to accompany the physical gesture.

Inquiries regarding anything one has learned about the person, the new baby, wife, mother, etc, are expected.

One does not get by with *Hola*. The tone of one's greeting is important. After three or more encounters, one must offer specifics by inquiring about some aspect of the person's life, such as How goes the work? the classes, the business, the trumpet lessons?

After regular contact, if one is just passing by, the above relaxes. One can revert to what's expected for the second meeting.

Children, having met an adult once or a hundred times, always kiss the person on the left cheek. One kisses them willingly for this delicious gesture.

Teenagers are expected to offer similar cordialities. Most do.

Upon leaving, one says *Ciao*, or *Ciao Ciao*.

Upon entering a shop, restaurant, or approaching a vendor, one always says *Buenas dias* or *Buenas tardes*, even if one is merely buying a bottle of water. Any interaction with a person who sells products requires respect. Cubans sense false cordiality immediately and will mock any form of snobbery. If one runs into the maid on the street, greetings and kisses are exchanged.

One never passes persons in a house in which one is staying without acknowledging each and all with a simple greeting of *Buenas dias*. It is not uncommon for the lady of the house, regardless of whether she's known you a day or a lifetime, to ask, *¿Como estas, mi amor?* Or *¿Como te vas, mi amor?*

One never bumps up against or brushes by another person on the street without saying *Disculpe* or *Disculpeme*.

However, manners on the telephone are more lax. One may answer a ringing phone with *¿Oigo? ¿Bueno? Digame*, and *Dime*. The last is reserved for callers with whom one is familiar. No jocularity is commonly used to answer a phone. However, when one is speaking to an anonymous operator at the national telecommunications agency, Etecsa, in an attempt to clear up some discrepancy, it is common to call the operator *Mi Vida*.

81

This phrase is often used between persons who are arguing and has replaced the more ideological *Companero*.

Arguments are often heated matches of reason and wit. *No es justo* is the classic rhetorical device, as Cubans are deeply sensitive about fairness. The object of a Cuban argument is not to win but to achieve a compromise in which there was *malos entendidos*, or some misunderstanding. Cubans talk on top of one another and often passersby will join in and speak for one side or the other. People will argue over what seems to be a small point, such as the exact number of base hits by a favorite batter. (The majority of Cubans have no access to the Internet for instant verification.) Retaining one's dignity and preserving the dignity of the other person are key. This, of course, does not exempt either party from residual bad feelings. "Oh yes, he's the one who screwed up, she insisted on, they demanded that," will serve as gossip for a while, along with barbed remarks upon seeing the other party once again. Who delivers a curt, *Tenga un buen dia, senor, si puede.*

Near Marvelous

by Maude Larke

It was only when I thought to write this that I realized that I was about to describe my FIRST time in the Alps. My FIRST, for God's sake. And it's now that I realize it.

1994. Finishing a year of teaching at the pathetic Université de Nice English Department. Nice is practically shoved into the sea by the Alps. It's a mostly uphill city. And behind it all that mounting freeness, creased, sharply folded, a crumpled mossy velvet cushion couching brown–white agates of surprising villages, perched or nestled through the hints or dictates of Roman road or Celtic water points. We rose into this upholstery along a thread that had been dropped onto it, a thin looping mountain road.

The road led to a refuge, the refuge sat at the foot of a thin, steep, zigzagging path, the path gave, just as we gave out, onto a pass and a vista that took in still lakes and the Italian border guessable by compass direction. Somewhere in this world there exists a photo of that expanse, with, in one corner, like Breughel's Icarus, the splayed starfish of my then partner.

A thin coating of human lies here and there in that abrupt wrinkle that lay beneath us, known as La Vallée des Merveilles, the Valley of Marvels. Some Paleolithic culture had swarmed there like lice on a medieval head. Little is left to show their presence but a set of shallow carvings on different rocks. Some are small, a little bigger than a hand (my hand hovers in another photo somewhere, demonstrating scale), but one takes up a mountainside. That one shows a face, and it is replicated by a smaller face carved into a vertical rock face that hugs one of the valley's paths. The others are hands or animals or seeming symbols, possibly the sun or moon or a witch. It was in order to discover these leavings, inside–out Lascaux, that we had attacked the upward zigzag. Now, after a pause and a snack, including a generous helping of dried apricots, we toed the lesser zigzag down.

That zigzag led to another refuge, on a lesser road curling arduously up from Italy. Because the Italians could arrive there in vehicles many of them did, without any planning but for road maps. Thus they began the guided visit as if they were walking down the via Roma in their respective towns. One such attempt at the visit was cut in half by the concerned guide when the small shoes began showing blood. We, in boots and even with staves, cameras slung closely, nearly danced over the rocky, nearly natural terrain.

On that trip we saw the scratchings, heard whatever explanations could be given in French and Italian, marveled at the marvels, photographed, and enjoyed the Alpine summer, sunny but comfortable from the altitude. My Nice tan took on more gold.

It was as we were leaving the raggedness, returning to the alpine prairie, curving along the last stretch and reach of rockface, that I noticed one key thing. Dried apricots do not stay dry. Especially when ingested in quantity. I stuffed myself as far back as possible in the last shallow vertical crag and, as my partner watched on the trail, I "dealt with the matter". A brief glance that she made to me while watching became a double–take, and once I had done "dealing", I saw why. I unearthed the nearest, most complaisant big rock sprouting alongside the path to spare the visitors at least the sight.

Farther through the meadow, we came across a woman dressed all in green. She asked us, "Do you have a bag of garbage?" My partner answered, "Yes", to which the woman asked, "Can I see it?" I was about to tell her that she could damn well think to carry empty bags herself, if she needed one, when my partner added, "We left it with our backpacks. We ate in the pass."

The woman nodded and moved on, we continued as well, and I asked my partner why she hadn't told that woman a thing or two (in her usual overly aggressive style). She explained that the woman was a Ranger, there to see that we didn't litter the national heritage. I didn't ask my partner how she knew.

This visit ended with dinner and a bunk at the refuge before making the return hike over the same pass the next day. Like the sheepfold found a year later dropped onto a more northern Alp and peeking down at La Grande Chartreuse (home of the liqueur), offering a real wealth of fondue (four different cheeses, three white wines), the refuge in La Vallée des Merveilles knew how to fill the inner hollows created by mountains. The most opulent carbonara, egg mounted in its halfshell, was served dish by dish, not in the negligent communal pot. Such hot richness did its soporific thing, and all the transitory travelers slumbered side by side in the dormitory that night. I don't remember any snoring, although it would have been fairly justified.

The next day we took on the gradual rise of the homeward journey. Partway up we heard a shrill, repeated sound. We had thought at first that it was a bird. This was an observation that I made the mistake of making in front of an ornithologist friend, who immediately developed a lengthy and detailed explanation.

"Certainly, a *martinet noir* could have been around, it does a scriiii–scriii sound, or perhaps the *torcol fourmillier*, it tends to a kei–kei–kei. The *pic épéichette* is more ki–ki–ki, not kei–kei–kei. What you described was too short for a *bergeronnette printanière*, it's rather tsip–tsip–tsip . . . " And on in that vein, with me only hoping desperately that I could at least remember the names so as to find them in English later. (Miraculously, I did: swift, wryneck, lesser spotted woodpecker, yellow wagtail, and of course she also imitated the honey buzzard, the goshawk, and the rock partridge, among many, many others. I was very careful never to mention birds in front of her again.)

As we rose, we saw a movement. It was in rhythm with the keening cry. It was *une marmotte*, an Alpine ground–hog. It was shouting. Smaller, more rapid movements taking up more space brought our attention to two small baby *marmottes* (marmettes?) chasing each other gleefully around the low hill on which the other – no doubt the mother – sat on her haunches and convulsed with each of her shouts. We made a few more steps, and she cut herself off mid–keen and dove into a hole just at her feet. As we came to the hole, the carousing of the young ones brought them to our feet. They stopped dead and stared up as we stared down. After a long, mutually immobile moment, they glanced at each other and plunged down the hole. We paused a moment longer, glanced at each other, continued our trek up.

I never saw *marmottes* so closely again. The nearest I have come is a Chamonix sweatshirt which has on the left breast one of the little furry things eating some very questionable green stuff. And also the gift of a *marmotte* puppet by my then third partner, whom I was told was named Cham. He went off for adoption to the French version of the Salvation Army five years later. I never had the pleasure of seeing innocent playful *marmottes* up close again.

And only just before I thought of writing this did I think that I could have tried to offer them a dried apricot.

A Matter of Faith

by D.M. Simone

Ruth Roman said that being in show business broke her heart more than once and yet she still loved to act. I open my e—mails and think about a woman I suddenly wish I had met. *Thanks for your submission but as a company we do not wish to be associated with such a grim topic.* I navigate my red marker over a list that hardly shows a spot of green. Another rejection and once again I wonder why Gail Patrick Jackson chose to produce rather than act on *Perry Mason.* Why, as a child, it had been so much easier to *imagine* than to now *be* a writer / producer with a degree in English.

I take a deep breath and close my eyes, breathing out a fleeting feeling of defeat before it overwhelms me. Radio Vintage is playing Cole Porter and I suddenly wish it was midnight and a taxi would arrive to take me back to my favorite decade, to a Hollywood that no longer exists. When the phone rings I dread picking it up. I'd rather continue my research on women in the Golden Age than face the financial dead end of a project I'm beginning to fear will never see the light of day.

"Did the charity come back to you about their involvement?" I shoot out my question before my head producer can take a breath to say hello.

"They need more time." Liz forwards their scanty message and I hear her stirring her morning coffee with so much force, I can almost taste the frustration she's trying hard to cover with a yawn. "How's your day job coming?"

"You know me, I've always wanted to be like Della Street." I shrug and laugh.

"Well, you have the style down to perfection." Liz talks through another yawn. "I'm sure you'll get the hang of the rest in no time."

"I've come to realize I'd rather have a Della than be one," I sigh more deeply than intended, allowing my thoughts another moment in a world of black and white.

"Any news from the crowd–funding guys?" Liz cuts in. I hear her fingers fly across the keyboard, typing as we speak.

"The usual." I quickly open their latest message. "*You are now ready to launch your project. Just two more steps to activate your campaign.*"

"What's missing now?" My producer rolls her eyes loud enough for me to hear.

"Our statement of purpose," I reply and duck for cover in anticipation of her reaction. It's the silence that surprises me. "We did submit it, weeks ago," I answer a question Liz didn't have to ask. "Same goes for the additional pictures they requested and the video. Everything's uploaded and in place. I really don't know why they keep us locked in that preparatory phase."

"Did you check back with them by phone?" Liz is all producer now, annoyed out of her wits.

"The only info they list is an e—mail. No direct contact," I apologize. "It's the same game all over again. Always back to the beginning."

I understand the muffled scream I hear on the other end of the line, the fake little sob that follows, the sound of a hand or head that thuds on a desk.

I use the moment to voice my frustration. "I don't think we should follow up with them. There are other platforms, other ways to close our funds." I don't know what else to say. Instead, I hear the clicking of her fingers on her keyboard, the sounds Liz makes when she's lost in thought.

I stare at my own screen, see our list of nos and maybes, the standard answer to our daily effort: *don't call us, we'll call you.* For a moment, Joan Davis crosses my mind and Lucille Ball, and I mentally bow to them for producing their own material a good sixty years ago, for having the stamina and courage, something I suddenly question I have.

"We have an offer," Liz interrupts my mood before it becomes depressing, her own enthusiasm tainted by too many faded glimmers of hope.

"Distributor or sponsor?" I ask, unable to produce a genuine smile.

"Equity investment." She sounds preoccupied. "I'll have to study this and come back to you later." Another second and the line is dead.

I slowly drop the receiver and put it on the cradle, and sit in silence for a while, my eyes lingering on research quotes and post—its framing my computer.

I glare at my screen and remember how Barbara Hale once told a reporter that she's been blessed in her life. Not for the first time I appreciate her answer and pray for a chance to soon be able to say the same.

Desperately Seeking Sustenance

by Gill Hoffs

It's hard to know in Scotland what's going to kill you first. A drunken bigot with a knife because you're wearing blue or green? Whitegoods tossed from the balcony of a high rise flat? Or the cuisine.

I remember going to a chip shop when I was about twelve years old and hungry.

"Can I have a mushroom pizza, please?"

"Naw, we don't dae pizzas with flavours."

"Eh? Why not?"

"The bits fall off."

"Fall off *where*?"

"Fall off in the fryer and mix with the chips."

In Scotland, the pizzas are deep–fried. Sometimes in batter, a kind of 'pizza tempura' but less healthy. We call it 'pizza crunch'. They're nothing a native Italian would recognise, especially once we've doused it in salt and vinegar.

The vinegar is something to be wary of, too. Not everywhere, just in the grimier estates and inner city areas. If you're visiting and there's a bottle of it on the counter, or even worse, on the tables if there's an area for 'sitting in', then don't whatever you do use *that* on your meal. Junkies sometimes – not always, but certainly more often than you'd like – use them to rinse their needles. I for one prefer my chips without a sprinkling of blood and residual smack.

It's better to risk having too little or too much vinegar, dumped on by the serving staff from their stash behind the counter, than turn cannibal without even knowing it.

I've learned that if I want to eat pizza, there's one way to be sure it's The Real Thing. If a takeaway makes proper pizza from stretchy dough, tomato paste, and loose cheese and toppings, they advertise it as a selling point – usually with a big neon sign. 'Oven Baked Pizza!'

It's the same with pies.

Sometimes they're fried in a crust of batter. Oil pools in the polystyrene tray the pie's served in. To make this dish palatable, we douse it in vinegar, so oil floats on top of the vinegar too. A half–inch of carbohydrate and fat coffins the kernel of gristly pink meat.

When I lived in the North of England, there was a thing known as a 'Wigan kebab'. I'd thought it would be something like a doner kebab (pitta bread or a tortilla wrap with a slice or two of spiced meat – usually reconstituted / repositioned lamb – from a vertical spit with shredded iceberg lettuce, raw onion, tomatoes and sauces) but with brown sauce instead of salsa and sour cream, and maybe some pickled onions in place of the doner's limp, wilting salad and unnaturally yellow sweetcorn.

A Wigan kebab's a meat pie trapped in a bread roll.

This is still healthier than the famed dinner of drunks, the Cheese–In–Burger. Two burgers sandwiched round a slab of orange Scottish cheddar, the whole thing dipped in batter, deep–fried, and served in a buttered roll with salt and sauce.

Feeling hungry yet?

How about dessert? We don't just have the semi–mythical deep–fried Mars Bar – battered, gooey, and oozing sweet sticky calories. Our sugariest confectionary has a quasi–medical name, possibly to get any regular consumers acclimatised to the hospital environment where they'll inevitably spend time, because of a bigot's knife, booze, drugs, or their diet.

Tablet is a crumbly version of fudge, or fudge is a chewy version of tablet – it depends where you're from. More than a bite of it will make your tonsils burn and your uvula twitch. A whole bar and you'll develop incredible thirst and thick scum on your teeth.

Sometimes that's a good thing. Plaque can cover cavities cheaper than any dentist, and if you don't like how the plaque's looking you can always brush it off.

Don't let any of this convince you that Scots don't enjoy their food – they love it. So much so that an empty fridge–freezer can lead to the aforementioned offending article being thrown from great heights in frustration. If it lands on you, it'll kill you. If you love your relatives, you'll leave something in your will for a wake. How about holding it in a chippy or the pub? A decent spread of meats, cheeses, and breads – all battered and deep–fried and called things like 'pizza' and 'burgers' and 'pies' – with a nod to the vegetable kingdom in the shape of chips and ketchup.

They can wash it all down with a lurid soft drink, a shandy, or a float: anything sweet, fizzy, and wet will do – a float is a drink with a dollop of ice cream on top.

If they're watching their figures, they'll make sure the soft drinks are diet.

Visions of The Saint

by Cheri Ause

Most people thought of Larry St. Clair as the guy at the end of the bar who'd wax philosophically, if not always coherently, to anyone within earshot or no one at all. Others, who claimed to know him better, pointed out the gaucho hat and dark plaid buttoned–to–the–throat raincoat, and how he'd twist a strand of shoulder–length hair around his middle finger when he talked. They explained it in one word: Vietnam. But Larry's friends from the old days knew The Saint had been bat shit crazy long before his boots ever hit the ground at Cam Ranh Bay.

They remembered way back in high school when they all worked at Brighton Lodge, pounding shots after work from fifths Larry pilfered from the dining room liquor cabinet. After stumbling to their cars, they'd convoy down Big Cottonwood, The Saint always in the lead. Barely holding the S–Curve at 50–plus, he lost it just that one time and lifted off, airborne over the second loop, plunging straight down into Mill B. They found him tangled in scrub oak, his kneecap busted, a cut over his right eye. Not so lucky his best friend Tim Fowler, Air Force Academy appointee who, sober enough to think Larry might not make it home, followed The Saint's tail lights into the night.

After the war, Larry saw *The Deer Hunter* six times; *Apocalypse Now,* three, then sat quiet while his combat–deferred friends opined on the war. Near the end, Saturday nights at his house meant bonfires in the front yard and firearms in the kitchen where he orchestrated alcohol–and–sensimilla–fueled shooting contests—a .22 pistol at ten paces from a poster of Richard Nixon hanging inside the back door.

He'd been gone a week before people started asking, then two weeks, a month. One Sunday afternoon he re–appeared at his usual spot along the bar just in time to catch the Broncos game. Close–shaven, wearing clean Levi's, a flannel shirt, and drinking tomato juice on the rocks, he talked about his new job at the copper mine, about the new woman he was seeing, about the small mercies of each new day.

Beggars

by John Wentworth Chapin

As I wind my way through Kandy, Sri Lanka, I go by the same spots every day, five days a week, and the beggars and I know each other. The beggars here usually sit quietly, maybe offering up a palm or rattling a cup. Sometimes a beggar will come onto a bus that is waiting to fill before departing. Most people will give a coin or two. The beggars of Kandy don't seem to resent either begging or their donors like American beggars do. You give a measly half a rupee and they bow to you. If you give a lot, they will sniff your hand. Yes, I said sniff.

There's Beggarwoman, who asks about my four—year—old son, Tucker; she's surrounded by a mass of filthy children, and when she was last pregnant, I found myself regularly handing her a healthy wad of cash. The new baby is a *cutie—pie*, although Beggarwoman says she is ugly and rotten because she's too dark—skinned. Beggarwoman is super chatty as well as being a big sniffer. I think she flirts with me. Sometimes I run into Beggarwoman around town when she's off the clock. She doesn't ask me for anything. We just chat or wave.

There's the old, grizzled, sailor—looking guy with an amputated leg; he is smiley and friendly and distinguished—looking, even shirtless and unshaven, propped on his blanket. Sometimes he hangs out with the scary four–toothed woman down the street who sells mothballs and betelnut and has breasts larger than Rottweilers. There's the double amputee with only one hand and leg apiece who waves and gives me the thumb up when I give him money. And the blind woman with the adorable little boy: she acts more blind than she is when you pass by. You can see her squinting into the cup afterwards, but it's not like she's putting on an act, because her life *sucks*, as far as I can tell. There are several men with legs horribly swollen by elephantiasis, laying like cut–down tree trunks across the sidewalk. The afflicted of Kandy put their afflictions on display, if they're poor. Since they are there every day, they are at least surviving – hunchbacks, dwarves, club–feet, albinos, and a few people whom I have been told are lepers.

This type of leper has polyps: strange, awful sacs of dangling flesh, like a child's marble inside a drooping pantyhose toe made of skin. I was on the bus one day with Tucker, and a man got on. He carried a can of paint in one hand; on that hand I noticed he had two small, dangling polyps. He was standing right next to me, reeking sourly, and I just wanted him not to touch me. Since I'm not even sure that he was a leper, and even less sure that I could contract it from touching him for a millisecond on the bus, I felt like a petty jerk. But when he moved to get off the bus – and closer to Tucker – I reached around him and quickly moved Tucker out of his way. Petty jerk or not, I couldn't stand still. I don't want to teach Tucker to be afraid of disfiguring infirmities, but neither do I want to have to send him off to a leper colony for school.

The other day, I was sitting alone at the very back of a bus waiting to fill so we could depart. Onto the bus came a leper – he is the worst case in town. I'd only seen him from a distance before, and he looks so awful that I always have to turn away. This poor man has polyps ranging in size from ball bearings to tangerines. Hundreds of them. They droop from his forehead, his nose, his eyelids, his cheeks, his neck; you can see them dangling from his scalp, under his matted black hair, from below his short sarong, from his knees and calves, from his feet, bouncing on the pavement next to his bare toes. He is the most horribly disfigured person I have ever seen. It's painful to me even to contemplate this poor man's life. I cannot look at him without feeling revulsion.

Then he opened his shirt, displaying his boiling skin to everyone seated on the bus: from neck to navel and elbow to elbow, he was a mass of fleshy bubbles that bobbled and swayed as he moved down the aisle toward me, begging for change.

I feel so much revulsion that I don't know what to do. I can't understand it. I almost despise him – for what? For displaying his awful body? For begging? For being poor? For being hideous? I don't know – I just want him to go away. I feel incredibly sorry for him, and I feel guilty that I despise him as much as I do. Under all that *mess* he is human. I would give him the small fortune of rupees in my wallet to put his shirt on and go away. But in order for me to do that, I would have to let him get near me.

I felt a rising, suffocating panic as he walked down the aisle toward me, displaying that ruined body. A sharp, unbearable combination of disgust and fear and guilt took my breath away. When he got halfway down the length of the bus, I bolted through the back door. Without even meaning to, before I even knew what I was doing, I was out of that bus and down the street. I kept walking, unable to get on another bus or flag down a taxi. I had to walk and walk and walk to rid myself of that bone–deep horror. When I'd finally rid myself of the horror, the only feeling I had left was shame, and I'm still trying to walk that one off.

Fly the Friendly Skies

by Michael Gillan Maxwell

The well—known slogan *fly the friendly skies* runs through my head as I board the monstrous plane that seats 10 across in coach. I'm in the middle of the plane, aisle seat in the center section, surrounded by a large group of public school teachers traveling to attend a conference. We're settling in for the six—hour flight from New York City to San Francisco.

As the last few passengers straggle in, a young man in T—shirt, jeans and sandals, with a short beard and unruly mop of curly hair passes by. He stops directly behind me, shoves his attaché case into the overhead compartment, and slides into the window seat across the aisle. He smells a little funky, as if he hasn't showered for a couple of days.

The attendant closes the curtain that separates first class from coach, as the last passenger to board walks up the aisle. The passenger is a young woman with lustrous shoulder—length black hair and hazel eyes, wearing a short, white sleeveless dress, nylons and red high heels. She's as glamorous as a runway model, and I don't think there's much chance she's traveling with the school teachers, but I can always hope. She's laden with glitzy shopping bags from various 5th Avenue stores and maneuvers up the aisle holding the bags in front of her. She apologizes for all the commotion, smiling and nodding her head at passengers as she passes by and heads for the center seat directly next to the man who just sat down. The aisle passenger gallantly volunteers to move to another available seat, so she'll have more room for all her things. Window Seat Guy looks delighted. He should be.

On the other hand, I'm crammed into my seat next to a dour and mountainous woman who's reading a Bible. The headphones clamped over her ears make it clear there'll be no small talk; which is fine with me since I'm seriously delinquent in my Bible studies. She's already claimed the armrest between us and is even spilling into my space. I briefly consider offering to switch seats with her to give her more room, but I realize I'd really be trapped and possibly crushed. I quickly change my mind and thumb through a magazine article about marijuana farming in Humboldt County. Window Seat Guy and Glamour Puss are chatting up a storm about all the wonderful things New York City has to offer. He helps by carefully tucking her shopping bags under the seats in front of them. I raise an eyebrow. I see where this is going. Lucky bastard, he gets Glamour Puss and I get lady wrestler who's giving off the vibe she'll bludgeon me to death with her Bible if I make one false move.

The plane takes off and climbs to cruising altitude. Passengers talk, read books, listen to music, work on their laptops or adjust the seat back and rest. Window Seat Guy and Glamour Puss lounge across all three seats like they're lying around in their living room. Ensconced in pillows and blankets, they're drinking wine and giggling themselves silly. Bible Lady is already fast asleep and snoring like a buzz saw, head lolling on her ample bosom. Every so often she stops. Dead Silence. While this may be preferable to the harsh rasping and gurgling, it's also disconcerting as I'm thinking she must have sleep apnea. This goes on for at least the next hour and I do my best to shut it out by eavesdropping on Window Seat Guy and Glamour Puss.

They're drinking more wine and carrying on about Broadway shows and shopping and restaurants and God knows what all. I sigh and go back to my magazine article profiling Humboldt County as the vanguard of high−octane marijuana farming in California.

It sounds like Bible Lady's breathing has stopped altogether. I'm alarmed enough to start mentally reviewing CPR and mouth− to−mouth resuscitation protocols. Just thinking about it makes me sick to my stomach. Still no sounds of breathing. I grit my teeth and lean closer. Just as I get my ear up to her face, she erupts with a violent snort and a loud gasp that sends spittle flying in all directions. I pull back so abruptly I bang my head on the seat in front of me.

Bible Lady settles back into a regular breathing pattern and I settle back into my seat. I notice her Bible has fallen off her lap. I gently pick it up and slide it into the seat pocket in front of her. I'm just starting to enjoy the quiet when I realize it's too quiet. There's no sound coming from Window Seat Guy and Glamour Puss. I know they can't possibly have sleep apnea too, so I turn to look. They're lip−locked, tongues down each other's throats. I jerk back around in disbelief, my mouth hanging open.

The other passengers stick their noses in books, snooze or watch the movie, which ironically enough, is *The Wild Wild West*. I whip open the magazine again and fix my eyes on the page, but I can't concentrate enough to read. The cabin is dark except for scattered reading lights and the flickering movie monitors. The other passengers are at least pretending to mind their own business. They read, do crossword puzzles, chat and do everything but pay attention to Window Seat Guy and Glamour Puss, who are now rustling around and muffling giggles as they rearrange themselves in the mountain of pillows and blankets. No way can I ignore this and I sneak a peek back to see what's going on.

Glamour Puss is sitting on Window Seat Guy's lap, facing him. They're wrapped in blankets doing their own interpretation of "the beast with two backs." Once again, I turn away in disbelief. Am I the only one who knows what's going on here? I can't believe Window Seat Guy got so lucky. That could be me back there, except he's the one with the cojones to reach out and grab a once−in−a−lifetime opportunity and I'm a rule follower. I'm a rule follower sitting next to a snoring giant who might be suffocating while Window Seat Guy gets to act like Caligula.

I eventually drift off until the captain's voice jolts me out of my slumber. "We've begun our descent to San Francisco International Airport and will be landing shortly. It's been a pleasure having you aboard." I look back to see the couple sleeping like babies. Window Seat Guy is resting his head upon Glamour Puss's shoulder with a blissful smile on his face. I shake my head as I turn back to fasten my seatbelt. I gotta hand it to the guy, I think, and actually chuckle out loud.

"Did I miss something funny?" Bible Lady asks.

"Oh good morning," I say, "I didn't realize you were awake. You certainly are a sound sleeper."

"I took a sleeping pill," she says. "It helps with my fear of flying. I could have slept through a hurricane. Did I miss anything?"

"Nope," I reply. "Just another long, quiet plane ride."

The plane arrives at the gate.

"I put your Bible in the seat pocket," I say. "I was afraid it would fall on the floor, and I didn't want to wake you."

"Oh that's sweet," Bible Lady says. "You didn't have to be so worried about disturbing me."

"Well, blessed are the meek."

Window Seat Guy and Glamour Puss stand in the aisle beside my seat like they've just been introduced at a cocktail party.

Glamour Puss says, "My name's Adriana. What's yours?"

"Josh," he replies. "Here's my card. Look me up if you're ever up my way. I'm an organic farmer up in Humboldt County."

They move a little way up the aisle.

"They seem like they'd make an awfully sweet couple," Bible Lady says.

I smile and nod as I stand up and move back in the aisle so she can exit. I see the graphics on Window Seat Guy's T–shirt: a marijuana leaf surrounded by the words, *Organic farmers do it in the dirt*. I'm still holding my magazine and toss it in the pile of blankets on Window Guy's empty seat.

There's That Noise Again

by S.B. Phoenix

It's somewhere to my right, though it's hard to hear through the thick cotton cage I wear on my head. I turn, the slight movement awakening a thousand little aches and pains that wake a thousand more. My eyes blur as I fight the desire to sleep and peer through the crevice in my search for the sound.

Tubes like chains fasten me to the mattress stiff against my back. The bed sheets are as white as the walls, tucked in tight at the corners, no ruffles, offensive creases removed with surgical precision. My head droops as a cackle shatters the silence, my body rigid with fear as my eyes source the noise.

It lies on the next bed, limp and lifeless on its back. It whimpers, and so do I.

Where am I?

I can't answer, my mind is numb with half–felt pain, but I know I've been here before. I turn away from the thing on the bed, fighting the urge to sleep a little longer, pulling against the sheets and drips that hold me down …

§

'*Don't move!*' My mouth tastes like cotton wool and my vision is dark and blurry, but I know better than to rise.

"Fix it later..." It's there by my side. Speech harsh and jagged, the words primal as it growls in my ear. The sharp prick of its forefinger pierces my skin and blood flows, fear shivers from every pore as it trickles down my arm.

I try to rise beneath the weight of the chains that anchor me. I catch a glimpse of the blonde mane that drapes its face and the look of hunger in its piercing blue eyes.

"Stay still," she growls again. My body snaps back, the chains hang limp though my mind rebels. It leans in close and strokes my throat, her hair against my neck as she bares her fangs preparing to strike and then ... she is gone. Tears stream down my cheeks beneath the cotton mask. My breath is short and raspy.

The man in the other bed jumps. He struggles as she approaches, squealing as it yanks the chains from his broken body. The squealing stops, the click of machinery takes its place and mustering my courage I turn my head and look.

Through the crevice I see the bed wheeled away, one arm dangling over the side, limp and lifeless as he's taken from the room ...

§

"Mr Phoenix, are you with us?" She has bright blue eyes and long blonde hair, she smiles and I feel my own mouth smiling back beneath the cotton bandage. I open my lips to speak but the pain is too much.

"I told you I'd fix this later ..." she whispers as she leans in close and her fingers widen the hole in the bandages, bright sunlight streaming into the open ward.

'There's that noise again,' my head says as the man in the other bed sighs.

The morphine drip beeps as his chest rises and falls, his eyes closed in sleep. Another prisoner at the mercy of his dreams ...

Which Way to the Vomitorium?

by Jane Hammons

Though I've lived in Berkeley for nearly 30 years, until recently, I had eaten at Chez Panisse only once—at a wedding reception back in the early '80s, shortly after moving here from New Mexico. At the time, I'd never heard of the restaurant, but the reverential tone with which people said *Chez Panisse* made me a little nervous as I tried to remember what the size and placement of forks signaled about how to proceed through a meal. When I saw that Chez Panisse was serving crawdaddies (the menu called them crayfish, but I know a crawdaddy when I see it), I relaxed. I didn't eat the ugly creatures when my brother fished them out of irrigation ditches back on our farm near Roswell, and I wasn't going to eat the one dangling delicately from my champagne flute. I was content to watch the wedding guests, cautiously but deferentially, munch mudbugs while sipping their bubbly.

My twenty-first century Chez Panisse experience, at the invitation of a friend and on her dime, began with an aperitif made with fennel, which I didn't much care for, but sipped earnestly the way I drink V–8—with the understanding that I will be transformed into a better person if I ingest the right things.

I like a lot of the right things. Growing up on a farm, I frequently picked meals straight out of the field in front of the house. For breakfast I might choose a cantaloupe, a couple of green chiles and a handful of tomatoes. Back in the kitchen, I'd quick—roast the chiles over the flame of a gas burner on the stove, peel them, and scrape out the seeds and membranes before putting them on a plate. After halving the cantaloupe and scooping out the seeds, I ate the melon from the rind with a spoon. The tomatoes I ate like apples, the sun—warmed juice running down my arm. I am familiar with garden fresh, locally grown produce. I own the *Chez Panisse Vegetables* cookbook. I know chicories from cardoons. Like any normal person, I like good food. But I do not worship it. And while I'd rather my food not contain deadly chemicals or be otherwise bad for me, I don't (apologies to Michael Pollan) research every meal.

After the aperitif came glasses of wine and four olives on a plate for my friend and I to share. A stingy little portion I feared might portend what was to come. But I couldn't have been more wrong.

My friend's empty aperitif glass was whisked away by the waiter, who let mine sit half full on the table even after he arrived with another glass of wine and a lovely endive and smoked haddock salad. The unfinished aperitif remained until the empty salad plates were removed, replaced by thick, crusty bread and little crocks of butter. The bountiful table was crowded and the constant serving and removing of plates made it hard to converse, which was the main reason I had accepted my friend's invitation. We hadn't seen each other in three years. In that time she had divorced and remarried. I was curious.

But after the bread, a shallow bowl of thick handmade pasta and fresh clams in a creamy sauce commanded our attention. Along with another glass of wine. It was Fish Friday and to be honest, I wasn't really looking forward to another fish dish. Maybe the problem is that I just don't like fish all that much. Or maybe the problem is Fish Friday. Dutifully, I ate the beautiful pasta and delicious clams, after which the main course arrived, accompanied by yet another glass of wine. A handsome, fist-sized piece of cod was flanked on one side by bright green leaves of sautéed spinach and on the other by a paler green mound of pureed artichokes, thick with garlic and cream. I lingered over the spinach, tasty in its simplicity.

If I'd been somewhere else, I would have asked the waiter for a go-bag. I am not your average size 14 American woman; however, I'm no petite thing. I know how to finish a meal. But I was feeling sick and wondered where my fellow diners were packing it away. Maybe, like those French women who Mireille Guiliano claims never get fat, they had a gastronomical secret.

When I asked the waiter not to serve me anymore wine, my friend smiled and said something about the decadence of the meal, which prompted me to ask her if she had ever seen *La Grande Bouffe*. She had not, so I made the mistake of explaining that it was a French movie in which a group of men repair to the countryside and eat themselves to death, while also destroying the household plumbing with their numerous trips to the toilet after gorging on beautiful cuts of meat, luscious fruits, crusty hunks of bread, vegetables in creamy sauces, cakes, pies, and other pastries, all prepared in a country kitchen. Unwilling to correlate what we were doing at Chez Panisse with the gluttony in the film, my friend smiled politely, looked away and commented on the hat a woman at the next table was wearing. But I had to wonder if Chez Panisse were required to print up the fats, carbs and calories on the menu board, how would this meal compare to one at McDonald's?

Having conjured images of Marcello Mastroianni, handsome as he was, groaning on the toilet, I was ready to go home. But no. A pretty crockery dish filled with pears and figs found its way to

111

the table. The fruit was soon joined by delicate slivers of cheese and thin slices of bread. This was preparation for dessert, a fig tart, which three hours earlier I had looked forward to.

By the time we were served an apple tart instead, I wasn't disappointed, I just thanked the lord that dessert had come at last. The tart was dressed up with a buttery scoop of something French that boiled down to homemade ice cream. I declined coffee thinking a liquid so warm and thick might make me hurl. Mindreader that he was, the waiter suggested a different beverage, another French concoction that turned out to be a warm lemon–flavored water in a clear pot full of bright green leaves served in small clear glasses. The presentation was beautiful, and if I hadn't been so stuffed, I'm sure I would have enjoyed more than its aroma. But I left my glass untouched and prayed for the meal to end.

Mercifully a tiny plate of petite star–shaped cookies and slivers of gold–flecked chocolate arrived. Like pep–permints served on the check tray, this signaled the end. As my friend paid the hefty bill and we got up to leave, I felt as though someone had taken my rib cage and spread it open with the Jaws of Life. I was in pain trying to contain all that I had eaten.

In 1923 Aldous Huxley was slapped with an *erron* citation by the OED for having misused the word vomitorium (it really means a passageway to a theater, not a place where decadent, overfed Romans puked their guts out in order to continue eating). Even knowing this, I engaged in a little erroneous thinking of my own when I stepped out onto Shattuck Avenue and wondered— which way to the vomitorium? I wasn't looking for a theater. I needed a place to heave my gourmet cookies.

Crack

by S.H. Gall

It's the kind of neighborhood where the bar above the hot dog stand functions as a drug warehouse. Lowest prices, biggest selection, friendliest – highest – associates. I live here, a block over in the midst of sushi places and frat boys, but I live here. I feel responsible for owning my surroundings. I like to drink. I like knowing there are cheap hot dogs downstairs for when the bar closes. I need to experience a new drug.

Walking up the steps to this bar is like walking into a den of sin. You might not find opium, but heroin is there; you might not find the mellow buzz of a dime bag of weed, but you'll find bags of crack like dollar bills, scattered on the bar, on the tables. And outside is an informal jitney stand – a series of black sedans illegally parked and ready to drive to the ghetto for a fix.

I didn't really enjoy smoking the rock, but I did learn some interesting facts. Many, if not most, of the black crack dealer population is on the down low. They have girls, kids, and a lot of sex with other black men. The pure gay black men get nothing but respect. "He never got a bitch pregnant, he knows what he needs, man, Rico is gay and happy." I put the pipe to my lips and suck, the bus comes, we get to my condo, suck the pipe some more. Then I'm sucking something much, much bigger. It takes less than a minute to direct the huge load of semen out of my mouth and into a black wad of pubes. When he leaves I'm minus my Creed cologne and an electric razor. But I go to bed fulfilled. In the most craven way.

There is value in knowing what can't control you, of course. By can't, I mean, it can have no more than one night's domination. Waking up in the morning, you take your psych meds, an aspirin maybe, many vitamins. I did this a handful of times and don't regret it at all. In grad school I did a lot more powder cocaine than I ever did the crack version, but I didn't ever need that either. These stimulants offered a very short−term rush. They improved different experiences − crack for sex and getting robbed, cocaine for a superhuman ability to socialize with everyone at parties. Who on earth wants to wake up and become a socialite Lothario at 6:30 AM?

I stuck with the vodka. I let it kill me, turn me, ruin me, and finally humanize me. Full circle, you could say, but I don't ever aspire to achieve anything but a partial disconnect.

Stoned

by Matt Potter

Was it the thump of his foot on the floor I heard first, or his low moan? I dipped my magazine and turned to look. We were three seats apart, and sitting in one of the many departure lounges at Paris's Charles de Gaulle Aeroport Terminal 1.

The man – soft linen suit, light brown hair and complexion now pale and sickly – bleated again. His wife – mid to late 30's and looking more Hispanic to me – bent towards him, speaking soft and low. Their two sons – nine and eleven? – stood aside, looking at their feet, looking out at planes on the runway, wide eyes aware their father was the growing centre of attention.

The man clutched his side, face twisted in pain, and slid further down the plastic seat.

And no one, including the man, looked like they understood what was happening. No hand wringing, just faces staring at fear.

But it was the noise next to me, desperate and primal and straight from the gut, that hit me most.

The man slid to the floor. Airport attendants whisked over, hovering above him, talking to his wife – they're probably asking him to tone it down, I thought, wondering if French was the wife's first language, and if she was able to communicate with the staff. Was he dying? they must be asking themselves. And why won't he stop groaning?

And then it struck me: the side−clutching, the floor−writhing, the limb−flailing − he could *not* keep still − and his inability to say anything beyond a moan.

Turning to my partner sitting opposite, "I think he's got kidney stones," I said.

And Daniel nodded. "That's the noise *you* make when *you've* got them."

I turned to look at the man again. Watching him twist on the floor was an out−of−body experience: I recognised his sounds and his actions but this time, they weren't mine.

The pain of kidney stones is intense, deep and insistent, like a sharp curved stone grinding into your organs. Crystals form over time in the kidneys. The pain is caused when the crystals − or stones − pass through the ureter, on their way out of the urinary system. Many people have stones and don't suffer pain as they pass. But when the stones are larger than the ureter, or large enough to scrape the sides of the ureter as they descend, then the pain is searing. The flailing and sinking and writhing and moaning is involuntary. You don't know you're doing these things. And only passing them − or drugs − can help. I've had them four times. If you are prone to them, keeping your system flushed, i.e. *drinking lots of water*, is the best prevention.

I've heard men say it's the worst pain they've ever experienced, and women who've had children say it's as bad or worse than childbirth. As the pain grinds away inside you and you're thrashing on the floor, or in a hospital bed, or in the back of a car, you think, unless you reach inside, through the skin and

116

muscle and wrench out your kidney, you'll surely die from the pain.

I did not know this man, his scared wife and his frightened children, but as I looked about the departure lounge at heads buried in magazines and newspapers and books, and faces turned away in the vain hope that somehow this human circus would disappear, I thought, *He probably doesn't know what's happening. So I'm probably the only one in this departure lounge who does know what's going on.*

And through all this moaning and whispering and hovering and wondering, I also saw, nothing was being achieved.

I don't speak French. I manage, "Bonjour, madame," when I walk into a patisserie, assuming my accent will give me away but my smile and my *bonhomie* when I say, "Bonjour, madame," will get me what I want. I can count – *une, deux, trois* – and say "Merci," and "au revoir" and "excusez moi" and "oui" (and "non" when I remember) and I do a lot of pointing and it's fun and I enjoy it, but it's just pretend really, it's just *acting*.

Yet watching him on the floor, his hand rattling the numbered departure lounge sign against which his body was now wedged, I knew something needed to be done.

I stood up and walked across to a desk. And clapped my hands. (Okay, I turned into my mother, who spent thirty years teaching young children. Maybe that's primal too.)

"This man is in pain," I said to the women behind the counter, pointing at him, playing the bossy English–speaking tourist, not attempting the slightest form of French. "He needs a doctor now."

"Yes, we have called one," one of the young women replied in English, eyebrows raised in surprise, perhaps because of the force behind my words, perhaps because she thought they had the situation covered. "Someone is coming."

"I think he has kidney stones," I said, clutching my side. "I've had them myself and they are really *really* _really_ painful."

"Yes, someone is coming."

"He needs a doctor now."

"Yes, someone is coming."

Should I apologise for the force of my words, I wondered. But then, well, sometimes you need to be forceful to get things done. And they didn't know me and I didn't know them and soon I would be flying off to Brussels ...

Looking behind me, I saw he still lay on the ground, and yes, two medical officers in green had just arrived and were talking to the wife and the children and the man and who knows, maybe achieving something.

Yes, something was being done.

I looked further up the concourse and, euros in hand, hurried off to the departure lounge bar. Then watching the Aeroport *medics* speak with the man and the wife and the still wide–eyed sons, I sat back in my plastic seat, and drank down the bottle of water I'd just bought, to keep my own kidneys flushed.

Ballerina

by Susan Tepper

When he used to love me we lived in an apartment 29 floors above the East River. Where I used to dance ballet for him. Wearing a black lace teddy. Barefoot across the parquet floors. I danced with my feet and legs and arms. My back and neck and fingers. Hair. Heart. My heart propelled a forty−something body into spins and dips and dives. Into a graceful Swan Lake. He sat on the couch smiling. How could he know. How could he know I also danced for every plane streaming toward LaGuardia. I danced for the passengers onboard. Making believe they could see my graceful swan. It was her glory days. Before her untimely demise. After all. Who could know I was dancing my future.

How to Forget

by Meghan K. Barnes

Drop out of school. Not because you're failing, but because everything there reminds you of him. Don't tell your teachers because they will ask, *What's wrong? Is this because of a boy?* Because as a freshman in college, it almost always is. Don't admit to your friends why you're leaving. Tell them you're failing out of school. Tell them you lied about your academic scholarship. Call an old boyfriend to drive five hours in the middle of the night to pick you up, and move you back home. Don't tell him why.

Live with your ex–boyfriend for a few weeks. Pretend the curves of his body match the curves you're missing. Accidently spill water on his cracked hands so they momentarily feel like the damp ones you're missing. Cook him food that you used to eat with *him* and get upset when your ex–boyfriend turns up his nose and refuses to even try. Read poetry the way you used to read it, before you understood the definition of *gone*. Be upset that he doesn't know what it's like to lose someone. Hate him for it. Move back in with your Mom.

Refuse to go to the church service, even though you already missed the funeral. Tell his mother something came up. Call his phone over and over, just to hear his voice, until his mother asks you to stop. Make a recording of his voicemail. Delete it and re-record it until it's not there anymore. Cry for the first time.

Go on a drinking spell. Start with tequila. Tequila was his favorite; you met over a bottle one night. Remember what it tasted like when he kissed you. Remember you were both dating other people, so you had to pretend it never happened. Remember sneaking away beside buildings, into bathrooms, behind shower curtains to kiss again. Miss him sneaking into your dorm room in the middle of the night just to sit with you until you fell back asleep. Remember how he never judged you for your nightmares.

Flip through your old notebooks, where he would leave you notes and drawings in the margins. Pore over the flip book he made out of your chemistry notebook. Smell the fading scent of the bubblegum ink pen he borrowed to do it. Wonder where it went. Wonder if it was in his pocket when he overdosed.

Blame yourself, because when you look back on it you know what he was planning. Drink more tequila and pour some on the floor for him. Laugh at yourself for wasting tequila. Feel bad for laughing, but remember that he told you he loved your laugh. Remember how he said you laughed like a little fat boy. Wish you could hear him say it now. Laugh at everything you can. Laugh out loud. Don't apologize for it. Laugh at inappropriate things like dead baby jokes and semi-serious injuries. Forget to remember sometimes. Throw away all of your notebooks (except for the chemistry one).

Fake a smile, but not your laugh.

Joyce to the World

by Thomas Sullivan

Two stuffed animals confront me when I walk into the grubby lobby of the Penske truck rental shop. One is a teddy bear, dressed in camouflage and clutching a tiny foam—rubber rifle. The second is a rat wearing a ninja costume and holding a club with a jagged ball hanging from its end. The animals stand at perfect attention and stare upward, challenging me to question the reading material displayed below the glass—covered counter. I look down at the text. Through thumbprints and coffee rings I read the words REPORTERS DON'T PROTECT THE CONSTITUTION, SOLDIERS DO!

That's funny, I could have sworn that Woodward and Bernstein of Watergate fame were reporters.

I shift my gaze down the counter, landing on a huge photo of two young men with enormous upper arms and ripped stomachs. Their olive t—shirts stretch and strain across their barrel chests like a botched skin graft. Both men stare at me harshly, as if to warn of the dire consequences that will result if I screw with the stuffed animals. I glance through the rest of the aggressive literature, which is filled with words spelled in capital letters and accentuated with long strings of exclamation points. I feel like I'm reading the comments section on a political web site.

Joyce, the office manager, enters our dimly lit room from a door in the back. A couple leaning against the wall in the chairless lobby slinks up to the counter. Joyce sighs and moans to no one in particular before saying, "The printer is misbehaving again... nothing new *there*."

A gloomy silence fills the room while I picture the brakes going out on the truck I just returned.

The female customer smiles at Joyce and says, "Hello." Her partner leans down to read the writing under the glass.

"We're here for a truck," the woman continues, "the last name is Jackson."

"Hmphh," Joyce replies without returning the greeting, "Jackson?"

Joyce turns away from the couple and starts digging through a tall stack of yellow forms. I sigh and look out at the parking lot. Through bent, dusty blinds I see Joyce's assistant squeezing his body between two trucks. Twenty or so trucks are jammed into the small lot at various angles, almost bursting onto the streets bordering this former gas station.

Joyce's voice brings my attention back into the room.

"So my uncle, he's a major, in Afghanistan. My grandson, he's a captain in Iraq. My husband *was* a major, but he's retired now."

The man and woman nod silently, probably wondering why they're being told this. I've heard a variation of this unsolicited speech a number of times already.

Joyce is just starting into the part about the others killed somewhere overseas when the male customer leans forward and says, "You know, I don't like the way some of these companies are supporting our troops over there."

I cringe. This is no place to provide input, even in support of the effort, because the customer is always wrong here at Penske. I lean against the counter and wait for the fireworks to start.

Joyce looks up from a form and stares at the guy. Her face quickly deflates into deep wrinkles, like a soccer ball losing half its air. She keeps staring silently as the guy takes a small step back from the counter, a sheepish look spreading across his face.

"Let me tell you something," Joyce says, blinking slowly over eyes with enormous bags, "If you haven't been there, you're not allowed to say anything."

I couldn't disagree more, but I'm not about to speak. Unlike this guy, I'm not giving up my right to remain silent. I just want to sign my release form and leave this unhappy place.

The guy's eyebrows rise in surprise.

"No, wait," he stammers, "I'm saying the companies are at fault here, *not* the troops."

Joyce isn't listening. She puts her hands on her hips and says, "You can't believe *anything* you see or read. My grandson says the reporters are all commies who wouldn't last a *day* in the desert."

Reporters are *such* pussies.

The guy raises his hands in front of his chest, signaling surrender.

Joyce barks "And you have *no* right to…"

I step in to the guy's defense. I clear my throat and say, "I know what you mean, ripping off the government, like those KBR showers that keep electrocuting the troops."

Joyce stops yelping and the guy lowers his hands to his side. The pair looks over at me with blank expressions. I quickly realize that this is probably not the best example, given the enlistment of Joyce's grandson. But no matter, the ranting has stopped. Perhaps now we can get back to the only reason we're all here, which is the renting and returning of trucks.

The guy grins at me with relief and steps back toward the wall. The tiny room remains filled with a glorious silence. Mission accomplished.

Joyce glares at me, her lips pressed together. We lock eyes for a moment. I'm preparing to be yelled at when Joyce spins away and returns to digging through the stack of paperwork. I'm pretty sure that the next time I have to pick up a truck here, I'll be getting the worst one in the lot.

The female customer sniffles and starts crying. She places a forearm on the counter–top and lowers her head.

"My son is heading to Iraq next month," she says, wiping away a tear.

Joyce looks up from her mountain of forms. She leans against the counter and places a hand over the woman's arm. In a soft voice she says, "Don't worry it'll all work out fine."

I turn away and pretend to be captivated by a safety manual at the other end of the counter, trying to provide these women with some semblance of privacy. The claustrophobic room with its single dirty fan feels like a coffin. A wave of guilt rushes through me for contributing to this innocent woman's emotional distress.

But this, it occurs to me, is the real face of war. It's not heroic, like that story about the college football star who skipped the NFL to serve his country would lead us to believe. It's not motivational, as the President wanted us to believe as he strutted

125

across that battleship, fluffing his ego. That stuff is just team—building mixed in with entertainment for the folks back home. No, the real face of war is two strangers feeling immense pain in a grimy, third—rate truck rental office. It's the stress in a woman who doesn't want to lose a son to a stranger whose mother doesn't want to lose hers either. It's that sinking feeling in the rest of us, standing around feeling helpless and powerless.

The teary woman and her partner stagger past me. Heading through the door the man rubs his partner's shoulder and says, "Here, let me drive the truck."

I watch the pair plod toward a truck with the man holding the woman's arm. I doubt they'll be joining the Penske Frequent Customer Awards Program any time soon.

Little Fish

by Joanne Jagoda

Real… to me is facing that I am getting older. I turn sixty two in a month. Ouch, that sounds really old. I saw *The Graduate* the other day and Mrs. Robinson, Anne Bancroft's character looked damn good and Dustin Hoffman seemed like a baby. I remember when Mrs. Robinson looked very old. I guess that's a bad sign, but I don't consider myself *old*. Is there a difference between old today in 2012 and old in say the 1960's?

Why I'm not old: I like music like the old Motown. I know all the songs—they were part of my teen years. I can tell you every single word to every Smokey Robinson song or song by The Supremes. And I'm still able to dance. Put Pink on and I can "get this party started…" I rock out. I love to dance and I'm pretty good at it. I even like some of the catchy dance songs today like *I Gotta Feeling* by the Black Eyed Peas. When I hear that song I dance around by myself.

Second reason I'm not old… I stay abreast of what's current. I navigate the internet, have an iPhone and Facebook account but I refuse to Tweet. I don't get why anyone cares whether I'm sitting in the audience at the American Idol concert or having a latte at Starbucks. I'll admit, I'm not sure I totally get the concept of the *Cloud*. Sometimes I still think there is a person sitting in a Google cubicle in Mountain View who is waiting eagerly to fulfill my information request for a recipe for blueberry and nectarine cobbler. The information available at my fingertips with a click or a swipe is mind—boggling to me.

Third reason I'm not old... I take care of myself. I exercise, spend way too much money hiding the gray in my hair, dress in nice clothes, even if not necessarily super—trendy.

When I got fed up with the ice pick management approach of my thirty—something boss, it was time to retire. She kept chipping away at me day after day until one day I just said *enough*. So there I was... out of work for the first time in years but fortunately not needing to look for a job. I had to figure out what to do with the rest of my life. I could only go to the gym so many days a week and realized I needed to reinvent myself as an active "retiree" doing meaningful things. I had already spent years as a community volunteer fulfilling various leadership positions so I didn't want to go that route again. I immediately signed up for tutoring at an elementary school where a friend worked and was assigned an eleven—year—old boy who had never been to school. I helped teach him how to read and that was very rewarding. I also volunteered to teach English as a second language to Chinese seniors—what a blast.

But something was still missing and I had an idea in the back of my head that maybe I should try writing. I cruised the internet and found a daytime workshop which was perfect, and there was an opening. The leader encouraged me to come and explained she used the *Amherst* method. There were eight of us and we'd write for two and a half hours to three prompts then read. The other members echoed back what they liked in a positive way. I was reluctant, nervous and felt like bolting when I walked in the first day. What the hell was I doing here? I remember the first prompt... "write about hair." After initially panicking, I wrote about my daughter's thick curly waist-length hair which has a life of its own. I was hooked. The words poured out like an unleashed river. It felt like I belonged right away and I realized there was a creative part of my soul that had been sorely neglected. It was as the Yiddish expression goes, *beshert*, meant to be.

I started writing every day and discovered a new world of writing contests, a plethora of literary websites and I cranked out short stories, poetry, memoir and non-fiction. Amazingly right from the beginning some of my pieces were accepted. I got "first place fiction" in a now defunct literary magazine for a fantasy story. I even got an honorable mention in the well-known Writer's Digest contest. So that wasn't *so* difficult. Ha! I learned that beginner's luck is no guarantee of future success and collect more than my share of rejection notices, some not even dignified by being sent on a full sheet of paper. Nonetheless I keep going, shooting darts all over and having enough positive feedback to keep me in the game. I liken myself to a seal that needs the little fish thrown to keep clapping and performing. I even fell into a small editing job for a poetry website through some of my writing ventures. As an added bonus, I've developed some lovely on-line relationships with people around the world I've met on my literary journey.

Sometimes I feel guilty that I am allowed this delicious pleasure of indulging my creative side by writing. When I think of my parents, their lives were totally different. They were never able to have the leisure that I enjoy to exercise or take classes or pursue interests. They came as immigrants from Nazi Germany, worked hard their whole lives and had their share of ups and downs.

There are also days I can't believe that I've been married for forty-one years. Now that we are both retired we face new challenges. We are fortunate that we laugh a lot and enjoy being together and traveling and doing the things we had put off. This is the time of life when if you are not friends with your partner and don't have fun together, you're in big trouble. One of the keys we've found is having your own interests and not being together constantly. My husband encourages my writing and is my first sounding board. I've read many pieces to him, and he likes them no matter what so it's not as though he's a harsh critic. He wants me to write a book. I tell him I'm not ready. He does his thing too. He has a regular schedule highlighted by volunteer work that he does as religiously as though he is being paid for it. He says he is going to "work" and loves what he does.

So real for me at my age is calling myself a "writer" and accepting that I'm in a new phase of life, but it can be better than any thing that's come before. As long as I'm able to keep my imagination flowing and put words down I will remain vital and young and keep that three-letter word "old" out of my vocabulary.

I Statements

by William Henderson

Dear _____,

I can tell you where I was when I realized I could—and probably would—love you. I was walking with several people, most of whom I had just met, to the venue where Tori Amos would perform later that night. No meet–and–greet with Tori Amos the day before, so we expected one, and were racing the clock. (I had wanted to go right to the venue; the others wanted to linger over lunch.)

We were at a red light, and the venue was in front of us, and I checked my email. You had written from outside of where you worked. Nothing much, this email (or maybe this email was really a text, because I don't have a copy of the email, even though I've saved all of the emails you've sent) but what you wrote was enough to let me know you were thinking about me. Before that red light turned green, I knew.

Knew I could. Knew I wanted to. Knew I was going to.

You and I had just met a few days earlier, after months of text messages and emails. Less than 48 hours spent together, and then

I had to go home, pack, and catch a plane to London. Two weeks in the UK before coming back home. Even then, you and I had no plans.

We'd make plans, we promised, once I returned.

We live 451 miles apart. The plans we'd make needed to account for the distance and the travel time and the arrangement of two lives that were –

Going along just fine?

We say that. Things were fine before. If we hadn't met, we wouldn't know what we'd be missing. Something else would have come up.

In London, reading you thinking about me, I wanted to stay in that moment, waiting for the light to change.

§

Dear _____,

That is one of the most beautiful things I've ever read, you say to me, letting me know the letter has arrived.

I hadn't planned on you commenting on the letters, not while I was still writing and sending them to you. Most of the letters I wrote quickly, since I decided I wouldn't edit. I printed each letter separately, put it in an envelope, labeled the envelope, stamped it, and on the back numbered it.

You save everything, you told me. You'll save these letters, and you'll save their envelopes, and my numbering will make re– reading the letters in the right order easier.

Only later did I think that the postmark would also have helped order the letters.

If I hadn't already memorized your address, I would have after this exercise.

Except your ZIP code. Each time I need to write it, I have to look at a picture I took of the first letter I sent to you in the mail.

You and I hadn't met. We had agreed to make each other a mixed CD. I made mine, and sent you a picture of the addressed and stamped envelope before I put it in the mail.

You let me know when it arrived, apologized for not having the time to make my CD, and two weeks later when you still hadn't made the CD, apologized again.

Three days before the weekend you and I planned to meet, in Buffalo where you live, I asked about that CD, for which I'd been waiting for nearly a month.

I thought I'd give it to you when you got here, you said.

I told you that would be fine, but really I wanted to tell you that if you didn't have the time to make a CD for me, then how could you possibly think you'd have the time for a long–distance relationship?

I almost didn't come. Me two years ago wouldn't have come, and probably wouldn't have explained my changing our plans. Let you figure it out on your own, would have been my approach.

That picture on my phone, how I remind myself of your ZIP code. Of how some decisions must not be made in haste.

133

§

Dear _____,

On your stomach, you sleep. Your head, turned to the left, toward the windows. The pattern of the pillow and its case, hatch marks on your cheek each morning. Your left ear, flattened. Your right arm, twisted above your head and under the pillow. Your feet, crossed at the ankle, right over left. The distance between elbow and shoulder blade, my view from my side of the bed.

Blinds cover windows, with gaps wide enough to let in some light in the morning. I'm awake first, and I count the shadows on your face.

No clock in the room – its ticking was loud, and all we wanted to do was stop or slow time, freezing moments that should last longer than they do – so time told by the way these shadows move.

Androids may (or may not) dream of electric sheep.

You may (or may not) dream at all.

I think about things to say to you when you're awake. And I think about memorizing lines of poetry, and reciting these lines of poetry, or maybe I think about copying lines from famous poems and sending these lines from famous poems to you.

(*I want to be with those who know secret things, or else alone.* – Rainer Maria Rilke)

(*But one man loved the pilgrim soul in you, and loved the sorrows of your changing face.* – William Butler Yeats)

The sentiments, if not the words, mine.

134

You, there, on your side of the bed, shadows on your face.

§

Dear _____,

I smell you for hours after I've left your home. Soap, mostly, the soap in your shower that you rubbed on my back. My fingers smell like you, or maybe you've worked yourself into the grooves of my fingerprints. Microscopic movements and motion, rubbing away what was and leaving behind what is. Your fingerprints on my body.

I wear your clothes most days. Shirts I've stolen, and some you've left behind, and one you've only loaned. (She looks like Gaga, Donatella does.) Some afternoons, when the kids are occupied and I don't have anything specific to do, I think about reorganizing my closet space to make room for you. Shelves and drawers and room on the clothes rack. Room in the refrigerator and freezer for the things that you eat, and room in the bathroom for your toiletries. A parking decal. Add you to my list of emergency contacts.

I smell you for hours after I've left your home, and then I don't smell you. I take a shower. I wash my clothes. I get used to sleeping alone. I don't always respond to your text messages. We seldom talk on the phone. We live separate lives, and I feel most in a relationship when you and I are together.

These letters, a clothesline, with you on your end and me on my end holding tin cans to our ears, trying to hear everything. The sound of the ocean, what you find inside shells, and what you find on opposite ends of a clothesline, ebbing and flowing. Tidal, this relationship.

135

§

Dear _____,

You, to me, middle of the day. You're on lunch, that hour you get every day when you walk home, sometimes take off your clothes, and eat. Grilled cheese or pasta, leftover pizza, cookies (when you have them). You tell me you reluctantly get dressed (you, naked at lunch, only on hot days when you feel like you need a shower after walking the eight blocks or so between where you work and where you live) and go back to work.

Your shoes, until you bought new ones, had holes in them, so your socks, on rainy days (because, even when you will get wet, you go home for lunch; a benefit to working where you work and living where you live) got wet, and your toes, in your wet socks, were often cold.

Still, you to me, middle of the day: If we were in school together, I'd pass you love notes in study hall.

I'm in my car, driving from place to place, getting done what I need to get done (perk of working where I work—my home—I can take off when I need to and get done what I need to get done, and though I am not often naked, if I want to be naked, I don't have to get dressed on anyone's timetable but my own).
I read your text and a response forms: If we had gone to school together, we wouldn't have dated each other.

Then another response: Would we walk together between classes with our hands in each other's back pockets?

Then another response: If we had gone to school together and dated, we wouldn't still be together.

Then another response: I would have convinced you to play hooky as often as possible by suggesting we stay at home and

136

watch John Hughes movies and other movies from that period of time. Happy endings. Stolen underwear. Everything, pretty as pink.

But I don't send any of those responses, because they came too quickly, and your initial text, middle of the day, probably didn't come as quickly, and you deserve to have as much thought put into my responses as you put into your statements.

Cause and effect, these text messages.

How about a picture of you naked next time, before you reluctantly get dressed? I'll respond with a picture of my own, suggestive enough that you'll have to take an extended break in the bathroom, careful, in there, not to get your shoes wet, sitting on that toilet, looking at the picture or pictures that I've sent.

facts

Author Profiles

Gessy Alvarez (*Notebooks*) grew up in New York City and New Jersey. Her fiction has appeared in *Thrice, Letras Caseras* and *Pank*. New stories and poems are forthcoming in *Apocrypha and Abstractions, Black Heart Magazine, Connotation Press, Lost in Thought*, and *Camroc Press Review*.

Cheri Ause (*Visions of The Saint*) was born in Ohio, and lived most of her life in Salt Lake City, where she married, raised two children, and taught English for 31 years. In 2010, she and her husband moved to the coast of northern California. Cheri's work has appeared in *The Redwood Coast Review, Fiction 365,* and *Every Day Poets*, among others.

Meghan K. Barnes (*How to Forget*) holds an MFA in non–fiction. Her book *For the Love of God* will be released in northern spring 2013. Her work has been featured in four anthologies: *So Long, Writers Block, Yes I can!* and *Thoreau's Rooster*, as well as multiple literary magazines. She has been nominated for the Pushcart Prize in both non–fiction and fiction.

Layla Blackwell (*Steps for My Uncle*) is a writer from Glasgow who feels utterly blessed to be able to live her dream. She is currently working on her first novel *Fallen from Grace*.

Laura Bogart's (*Fairytale*) work has appeared in *34th Parallel, Glossolalia, Milk Sugar Literatur* and *Full of Crow*, among others. She was awarded a Grace Paley Fellowship by the Juniper Institute at UMass Amherst. She is a featured writer on *The Nervous Breakdown* and is currently working on a novel.

John Wentworth Chapin (*Beggars*) lives and writes in Baltimore, Maryland, USA, where the water is always close enough to feel right.

Rebecca Chekouras (*Malcolmina XOX*) lives in an old iron works factory in the seaport city of Oakland, California. Her work has been published in the *San Francisco Chronicle, Curve Magazine*, and by the University of Wisconsin Press. She has twice been shortlisted for the Astraea Foundation fiction prize.

James Claffey (*spreading from the false fly*) hails from County Westmeath, Ireland, and lives on an avocado ranch in Carpinteria, CA, with his wife, the writer and artist Maureen Foley, their daughter Maisie, and Australian cattle–dog Rua. His work appears in many places including the *New Orleans Review, Elimae, NAP, Connotation Press*, and *A–Minor Magazine*.

Mira Desai (*Beholden*) lives in Mumbai where she works in the pharmaceutical industry. She writes fiction and poetry, and translates Gujarati fiction. She is a member of the internet writing workshop, IWW.

Joanna Delooze (*Itch*) is an ex–pat New Yorker living in northwest England with her Limey husband, two wild sons and a Border Collie, all of whom keep her from regularly writing. She loves all things cake related, writing and reading related, and in an ideal world would live and write in a cake shop on a cliff, overlooking the sea.

Gloria Frym (*Greetings from Havana*) is the author of two collections of short stories – *Distance No Object* (City Lights Books), and *How I Learned* (Coffee House Press). Her most recent books of poetry are *Mind Over Matter* (BlazeVOX, 2011) and *Any Time Soon* (Little Red Leaves, 2010). She teaches at California College of the Arts in the Bay Area.

S.H. Gall (*Crack*) primarily writes flash fiction. His work can be found in such diverse markets as *SmokeLong Quarterly*, *decomP MagazinE*, *Metazen*, *Nanoism*, *Monkeybicycle*, and *fwriction: review*, to name a few. He is reviewed in *Five Star Literary Stories*, and unpublished pieces can be found on *Fictionaut*.

Cinda Gibbon (*Enough*) is a writer, artist, and photographer in Gettysburg, Pennsylvania, USA. She was formerly a college librarian and has published and presented at national conferences in the fields of library science and management. Because of a chronic illness, she has taken an early retirement.

Walter Giersbach's (*Immortality, Version 2.0*) fiction has appeared in *Bewildering Stories, Big Pulp, Corner Club Press, Every Day Fiction, Gumshoe Review, OG Short Fiction, Over My Dead Body, Pif Magazine, Pill Hill Press, Pulp Modern,* and other print and online publications. He also writes on military history and social phenomena. *Cruising the Green of Second Avenue* – two volumes of short stories – are available at Barnes & Noble and other retailers.

Jane Hammons (*Which Way to the Vomitorium?*) teaches writing at UC Berkeley. She has a story in *Hint Fiction* (W. W. Norton) and is the recipient of a Derringer Award from the Short Mystery Fiction Society. Her writing has appeared in various magazines: *Columbia Journalism Review, Crimespree Magazine, San Francisco Chronicle Magazine* and *Verbicide*.

William Henderson (*I Statements*) is a Boston, Mass.–based writer who writes about love. He is included in several print anthologies, including *Best Gay Writing 2012*. He can be found at http://hendersonhouseofcards.com/ and on Twitter, @Avesdad

Gill Hoffs (*Desperately Seeking Sustenance*) lives with her family and Coraline Cat on a wet and windy hill by the Scottish coast. Her fiction and nonfiction is widely available online and in print, and her first book *Wild: a collection* is out now from *Pure Slush*. All links are available at http://gillhoffs.wordpress.com/

Claire Ibarra (*Things Left Behind*) is a writer, poet and photographer living in Miami, Florida. Her work has appeared in numerous literary journals and anthologies, including *An Honest Lie, Boston Literary Magazine, Amoskeag*, and *The MacGuffin*. Claire and her husband also own a hostel in the Peruvian Andes, en route to the Choquequirau ruins. You can learn more at http://www.claireibarra.com/

Joanne Jagoda (*Little Fish*) is a late bloomer when it comes to creative writing, as she only began in 2009 upon retirement at age 59, when she discovered inspiring writing workshops and classes. Since then, she has published a number of short stories, poetry and memoir pieces in online publications and print anthologies.

Maude Larke (*Near Marvelous*) has returned to writing after years in universities analyzing others' texts and films, and to classical music as an ardent amateur, after fifteen years of piano and voice in her youth. She was the winner of the 2011 *PhatSalmon Poetry Prize* and the 2012 *Swale Life Poetry Competition*.

Michael Gillan Maxwell (*Fly the Friendly Skies*) is a teller of tales, singer of songs, artist, musician, environmentalist, teacher and animal lover. He's prone to random outbursts and may

144

spontaneously combust or break into song at any moment. Maxwell's recent work has appeared in *Thunderclap Magazine, Orion headless* and *Short, Fast and Deadly.*

S.B. Phoenix (*There's That Noise Again*) is a writer, musician and dreamer and you can find his blog here: http://www.sbphoenix.blogspot.co.uk

Matt Potter (*Stoned*) is an Australian−born writer who keeps part of his psyche in Berlin. Matt has been published in various places online, his anthology *Vestal Aversion* was published earlier in 2012, and he is, rather amazingly, also the founding editor of *Pure Slush.* You can find more of his work at http://mattcpotter.webs.com/

Mark Rosenblum (*Indelible Impression*) − a New York native who now lives in Southern California − misses the taste of real pizza and good deli food. His work appears in *Tiferet Journal, Boston Literary Magazine, Everyday Fiction, Six Minute Magazine, Short, Fast & Deadly, Sleet Magazine, Monkeybicycle, Pure Slush* online, *Apocrypha and Abstractions* and *Penduline.*

Shane Simmons (*A Curious Fellow*) is a self−confessed coffee shop writer who believes that regardless of quality, each paragraph penned should be rewarded with sweet treats (cake, muffins, Belgian waffles, etc). London−born, he ran away to Glasgow ten years ago, expanded his waistline and now blogs at http://scribblingsimmons.wordpress.com/

D.M. Simone (*A Matter of Faith*) lives, breathes and works in film. She loves to write short stories, novels, screenplays and the occasional odd poem and is a frequent blogger on Wordpress where she savors her love of Vintage Hollywood at *Talking Classics* and explores her creativity at *Della's Notepad.* You can find *Talking Classics* at http://talkingclassics.wordpress.com/ and *Della's Note−pad* at http://dellasnotepad.wordpress.com/.

145

Jonathan Slusher (*Magic French Words*) is a stay–at–home father / part–time writer living on the foggy side of the Santa Cruz Mountains. He has an MS in Environmental Science, a German wife, and a South Jersey accent. Jonathan's short stories have been published in *Pure Slush* online, *Bartleby Snopes*, *Toasted Cheese Literary Journal*, *Paper Darts Magazine*, and *The Battered Suitcase*. He has also appeared on NPR Radio's Perspectives. His website can be found at http://www.waterlanding.net/

Sharon Louise Stephenson (*Where Her Mind Is*) has recently begun writing literary nonfiction. Her work has appeared in *The Dead Mule* and online @ *Pure Slush*. She is a professor of physics at Gettysburg College.

Thomas Sullivan (*Joyce to the World*) is the author of *Life In The Slow Lane*, a humor memoir about teaching driver education to teenagers. For more about this title visit http://thomassullivanhumor.com. Thomas is also on Twitter at @ThomasSullivan4.

Susan Tepper (*Ballerina*), a fiction writer and poet, is the author of four published books. Her recent title *From the Umberplatzen* is a quirky love story set in Germany and told in linked–flash. Tepper has been nominated 9 times for the Pushcart Prize. Her novel *What May Have Been* (Cervena Barva Press, 2010) was nominated for a Pulitzer.

Diana J. Wynne (*The Rose*) always tells the truth, even when it hurts. Her stories have appeared in the *New York Times*, *Mississippi Review*, *storySouth*, *Blueprint Review*, *Raw Story*, and online @ *Pure Slush*. She lives in San Francisco. Make her an offer.